WORKBOOK

HIRAGANA

in 48 minutes

ERI TOMITA-HARVEY | JULIE DEVINE

Hiragana in 48 minutes workbook
1st Edition
Julie Devine
Eri Tomita-Harvey

Publishing editor: Catriona McKenzie and Julie McArthur
Project editor: Simon Tomlin
Editor: Carla Morris
Art direction: Aisling Gallagher
Cover image: Shutterstock.com / Elena Zolotukhina
Cover design: Aisling Gallagher
Text design: Aisling Gallagher
Illustrations by: Makoto Koji
Permissions researcher: Kaitlin Jordan
Production controller: Karen Young
Typeset by: Nikki M Group Pty Ltd

For product information and technology assistance,
in Australia call **1300 790 853**;
in New Zealand call **0800 449 725**

For permission to use material from this text or product, please email **aust.permissions@cengage.com**

ISBN 978 0 17 040394 8

Cengage Learning Australia
Level 7, 80 Dorcas Street
South Melbourne, Victoria Australia 3205

Cengage Learning New Zealand
Unit 4B Rosedale Office Park
331 Rosedale Road, Albany, North Shore 0632, NZ

For learning solutions, visit **cengage.com.au**

Printed in China by 1010 Printing International Limited
10 11 25

CONTENTS

About the series *Hiragana in 48 minutes*

Hiragana in 48 minutes is the most widely used resource for teaching Japanese syllabary to beginning students of Japanese in Australia. Its effective method uses mnemonic flashcards and is supported by a teacher guide that provides a step-by-step guide to planning and presentation.

Workbook

This workbook supports the *Hiragana in 48 minutes* flashcards and teacher guide. It provides comprehensive *hiragana* reading and writing practice in an easy-to-use, engaging and structured format.

The opening exercise for each unit allows students to practise the correct formation of each *hiragana* and ensure balance within the squares. When a character changes its appearance according to a different font, it is shown at the end of the first practice row in a shaded square.

The wide range of activities, including dictation exercises for every level, consolidates and reinforces the learning of the script. Where appropriate, answers are included at the back of this book.

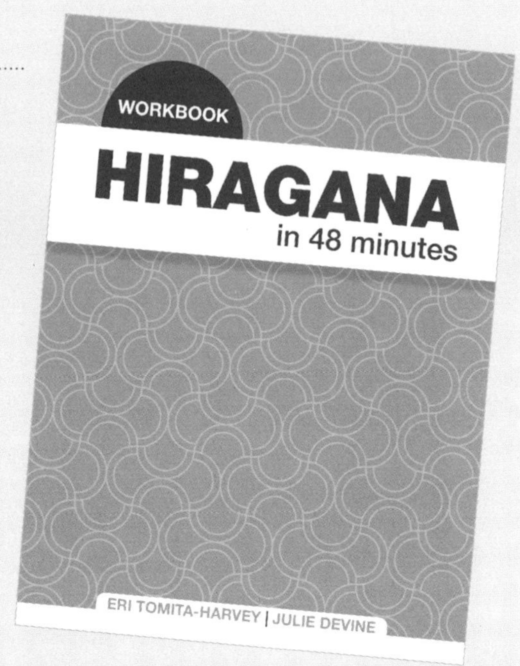

The workbook can be used in class or independently at home.

Nelson Languages website – free interactive resources!

Dictation videos can be found on the Nelson Languages website at www.nelsonnet.com.au/free-resources/nelson-languages. It is suggested that students complete the dictation exercises in the workbook for practice.

Quizzes and answers are also available. Contact your education consultant for access and conditions.

ISBN 9780170403948

Level 1: あ to お

1. Practise writing the Level 1 *hiragana* in the squares. Use the dotted lines to help you balance your characters in the squares.

Hiragana	Memory aid	Practice	
あ **a**	あ an antenn**a** is **u**p on the roof	あ	
い **i**	い Hawa**ii**	い	
う **u**	う **oo**ph!	う	う
え **e**	え **e**xtra dot	え	
お **o**	お **o**n the green	お お	お

ISBN 9780170403948

2 Use coloured pens or pencils to colour in the matching pairs.

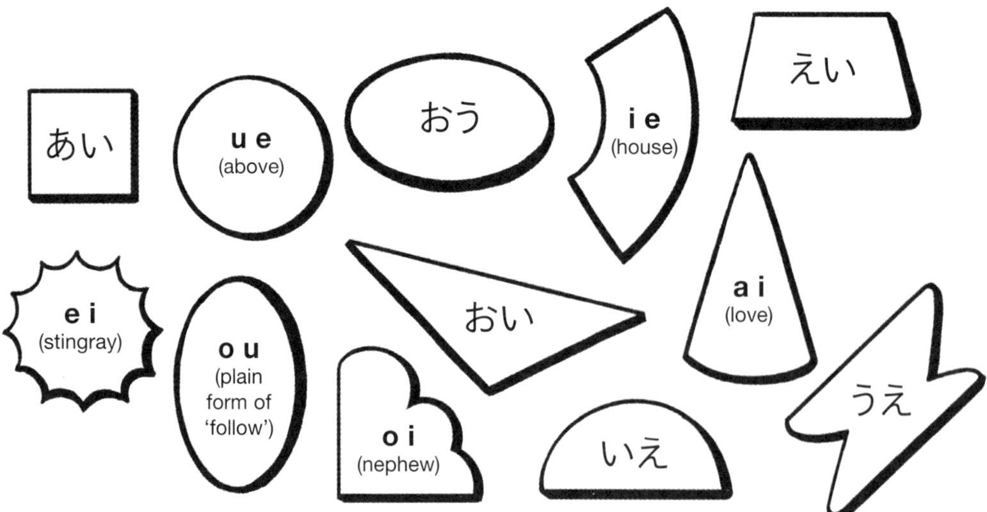

3 Write the words in *hiragana*.

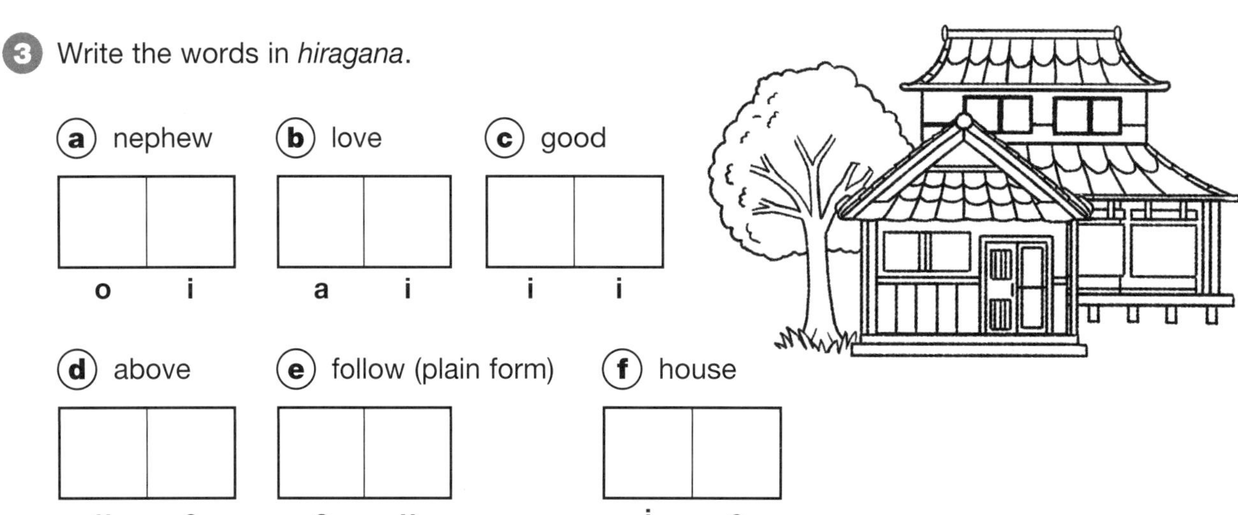

4 Listen to your teacher or watch the Level 1 dictation video. Write the words in *hiragana* in the first squares as you hear them. Then, use the extra squares to practise writing the words again.

a

b

c

d

e

ISBN 9780170403948

Level 2: か to こ

2

1 Practise writing the Level 2 *hiragana* in the squares. Use the dotted lines to help you balance your characters in the squares.

か	か	つ	カ	か			
ka	cut						
き	き	一	二	き	き		き
ki	key						
く		く					く
ku	cuckoo						
け	け	l	l一	け			
ke	keg						
こ	こ	¬	こ				
ko	cost						

ISBN 9780170403948

2 Cross out the extra *hiragana* to spell the words correctly.

ⓐ **ka o** (face) かおけ

ⓑ **i ke** (pond) いくけ

ⓒ **ki ku** (plain form of 'listen') けきく

ⓓ **a ka** (red) あかき

ⓔ **ku i** (stake, post) くうい

ⓕ **ko e** (voice) いこえ

ⓖ **o ka** (hill) あおか

ⓗ **ka ki** (persimmon) かさき

3 Find your way through the puzzle from あ to こ. The *hiragana* sequence from あ to こ is repeated twice. When you get to the first こ, the next one will be あ, followed by い, and so on.

You can move in any direction, including diagonally.

Start ↓

あ	い	う	あ	か	き	く	け	あ	お	く	か
い	お	お	え	え	う	か	あ	お	か	う	え
え	い	う	い	お	か	こ	く	か	き	く	け
お	う	え	い	い	け	き	け	い	く	こ	え
か	あ	え	け	こ	こ	く	う	え	お	か	あ
か	う	い	お	こ	け	え	き	い	き	か	お
い	か	え	き	あ	い	か	え	お	け	き	い
け	く	お	う	け	き	う	こ	く	か	あ	け
う	い	お	あ	い	あ	お	き	う	う	き	お
く	こ	か	け	け	え	こ	き	お	か	く	え
あ	け	く	う	え	お	こ	け	き	あ	こ	け
う	え	お	け	く	い	お	あ	い	お	き	こ

↓ **Goal**

ISBN 9780170403948

4 Write the words in *hiragana*.

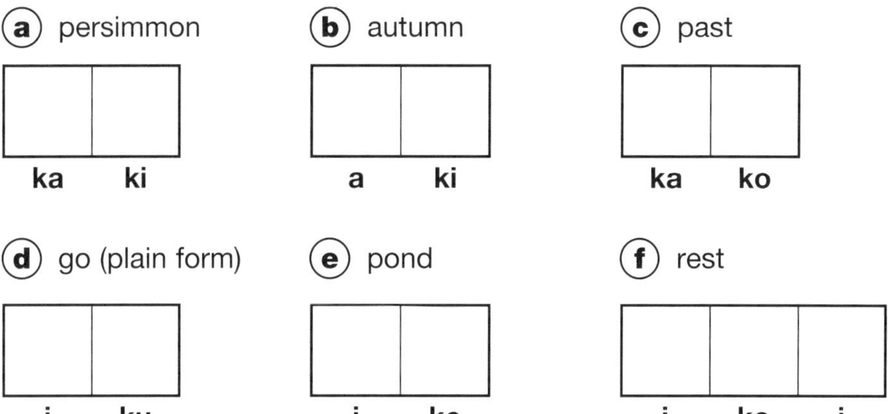

5 Write the words in the squares. Notice how you can make different words with the same *hiragana*.

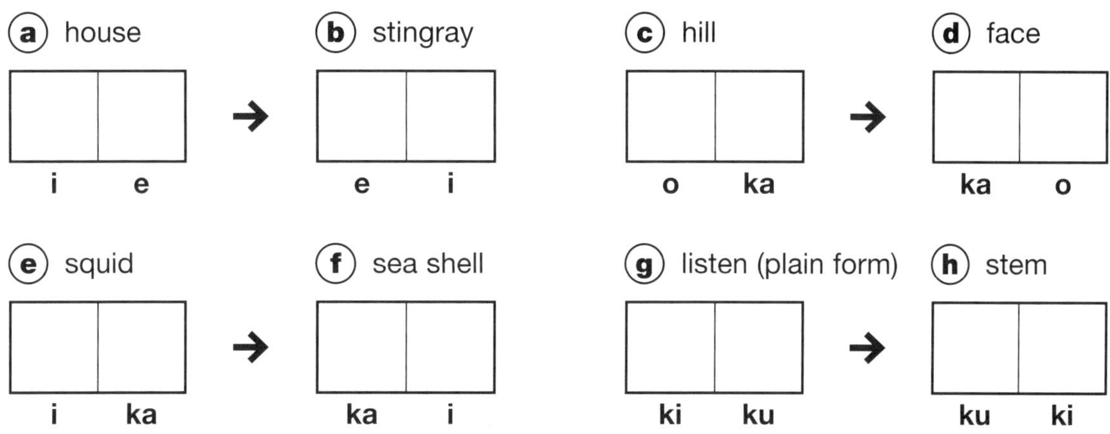

6 Listen to your teacher or watch the Level 2 dictation video. Write the words in *hiragana* in the first squares as you hear them. Then, use the extra squares to practise writing the words again.

ISBN 9780170403948

Level 3: が to ご

1 Practise writing the Level 3 *hiragana* in the squares. Use the dotted lines to help you balance your characters in the squares.

The symbol ゛ is written to the upper-right of some *hiragana*. It indicates that you are to 'voice' the sound. In other words, you tense your throat a little as you say the first sound. For example, with the characters on this page, a *k* sound becomes a *g* sound, so *ka* becomes *ga*, and *ki* becomes *gi*.

To help you to remember, think of **keg**.

The symbol ゛ has a few names. The formal name is *dakuten*, but Japanese people also call it *tenten*.

ISBN 9780170403948

2 Circle or highlight the words in the grid.

(a) **ga i ko ku** (foreign country)

(b) **go go** (afternoon)

(c) **ke ga** (injury)

(d) **ka ga ku** (science)

(e) **ge ki** (drama, play)

が	え	げ	き
け	い	ご	ぐ
き	ご	こ	ぎ
い	か	が	く

3 Write the words in *hiragana*.

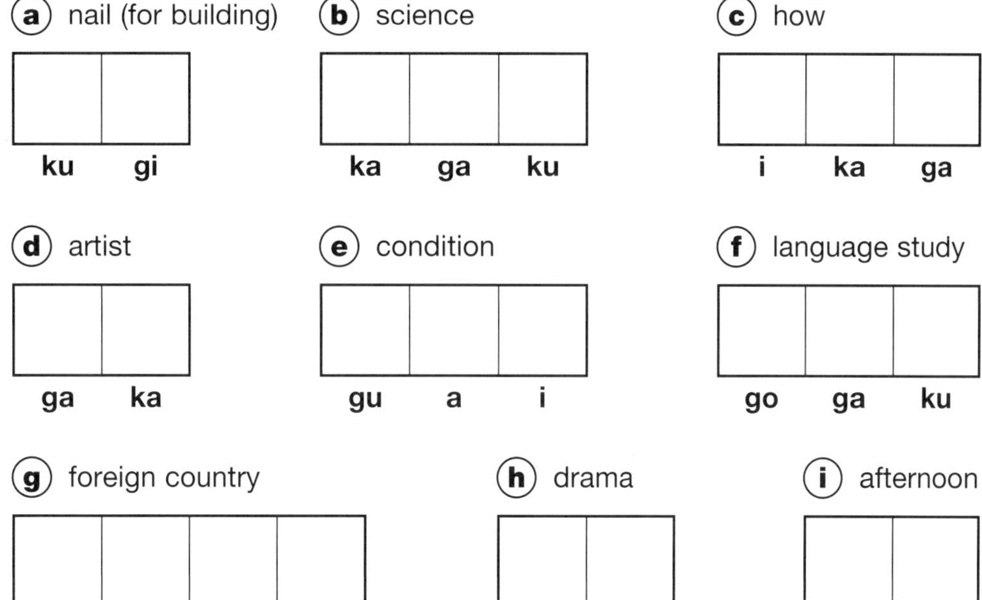

4 Listen to your teacher or watch the Level 3 dictation video. Write the words in *hiragana* in the first squares as you hear them. Then, use the extra squares to practise writing the words again.

3

ISBN 9780170403948

Level 4: さ to そ

1. Practise writing the Level 4 *hiragana* in the squares. Use the dotted lines to help you balance your characters in the squares.

Hiragana	Mnemonic	Practice
さ sa	**sa**murai sword	さ
し shi	**she**	し
す su	**soo**n	す
せ se	**se**tting sun	せ
そ so	**so**ft	そ

ISBN 9780170403948

2 Draw lines connecting the letters from left to right to spell out the words pictured. The first one has been done for you.

3 Complete each *hiragana* by adding the missing stroke.

4 Listen to your teacher or watch the Level 4 dictation video. Write the words in *hiragana* in the first squares as you hear them. Then, use the extra squares to practise writing the words again.

4

ISBN 9780170403948

5 Write each word in *hiragana*. Then, find each one in the puzzle. You will find them in every direction, including diagonally and backwards.

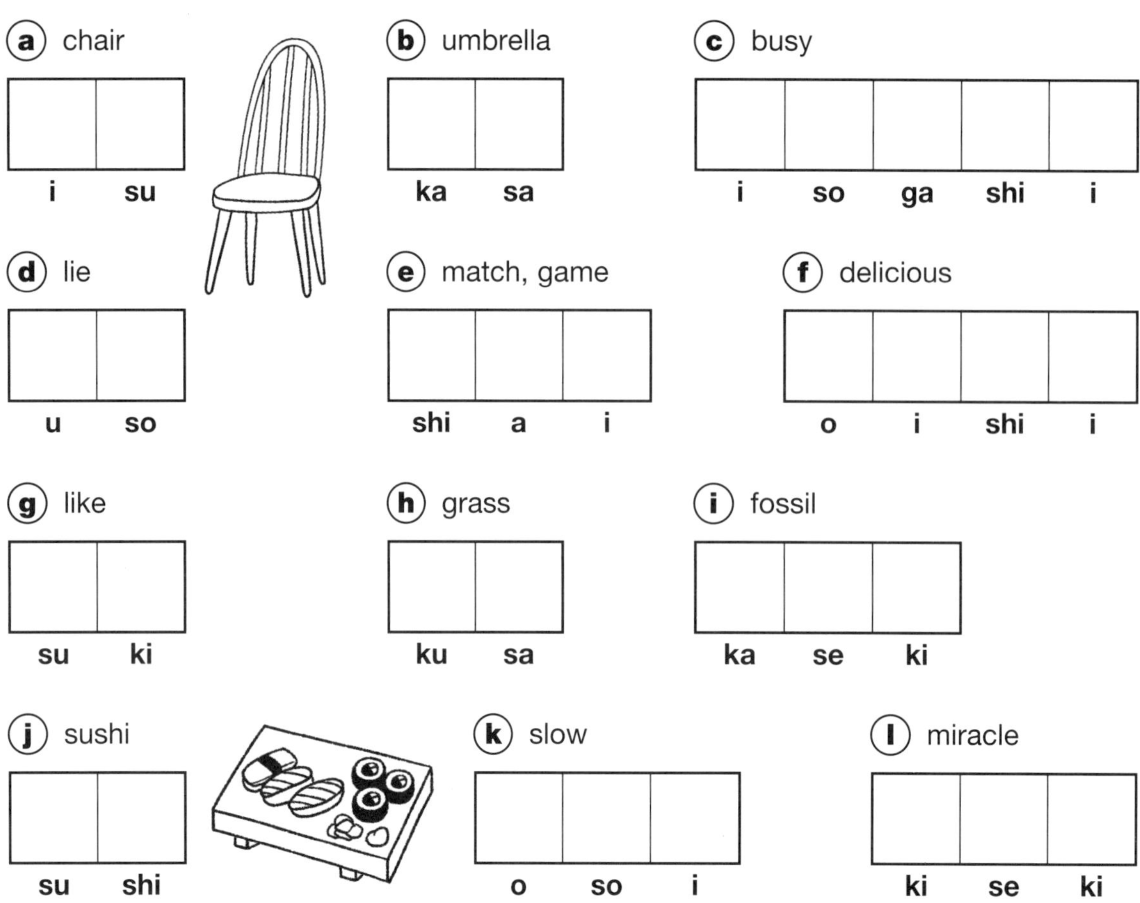

a) chair — i su
b) umbrella — ka sa
c) busy — i so ga shi i
d) lie — u so
e) match, game — shi a i
f) delicious — o i shi i
g) like — su ki
h) grass — ku sa
i) fossil — ka se ki
j) sushi — su shi
k) slow — o so i
l) miracle — ki se ki

い	す	あ	し	か	さ	お	か	う	し	あ	い
か	お	こ	お	け	こ	あ	か	こ	え	か	け
く	す	し	い	う	き	せ	け	す	け	そ	し
ご	え	け	し	ぐ	き	ぎ	い	き	そ	い	し
か	し	ご	い	く	き	あ	げ	け	い	そ	け
い	け	ぎ	あ	け	い	せ	そ	お	え	が	お
そ	け	し	せ	い	さ	ず	き	き	せ	し	が
お	さ	く	お	え	う	そ	せ	い	げ	い	い

ISBN 9780170403948

Level 5: ざ to ぞ

1. Practise writing the Level 5 *hiragana* in the squares. Use the dotted lines to help you balance your characters in the squares.

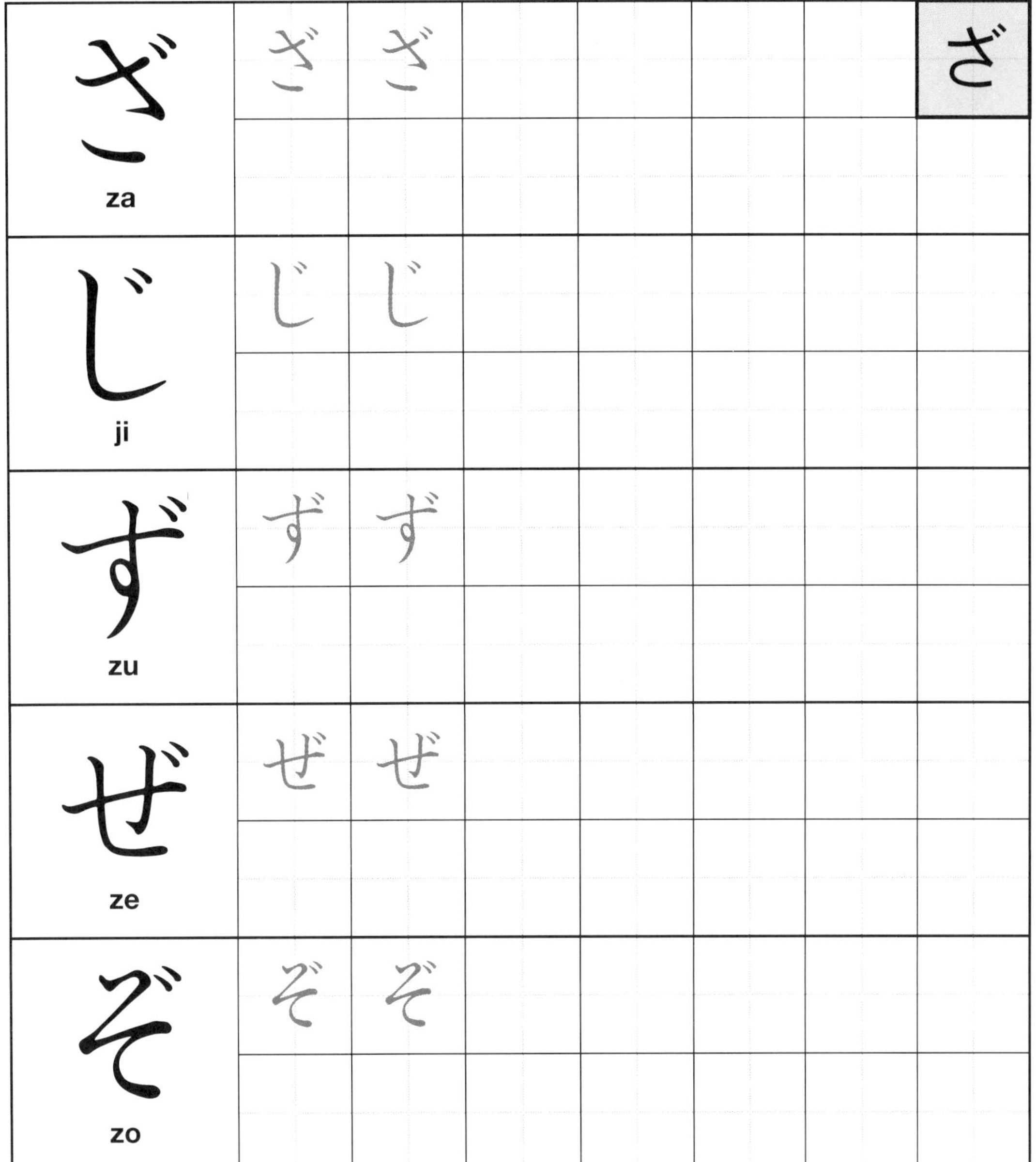

When ゛ is added to the upper-right of *hiragana* in the s line, they are pronounced with a *z* sound. For example, *sa* becomes *za*, and *su* becomes *zu*. Watch out for *shi* as it becomes *ji*.

To help you remember, think of the girl's name **S**u**z**ie or ***s**u**z**ume*, the Japanese word for sparrow.

ISBN 9780170403948

2 Choose the correct spelling for each word.

(a) **za se ki** (seat)	(b) **a ji** (taste)	(c) **ji zo ku** (continuation)	(d) **u zu** (whirlpool)
さぜき	あし	じそく	うす
ざぜき	おじ	しくぞ	すう
ざせき	あじ	じぞく	ずう
させき	おし	しぞく	うず

3 Write the words in *hiragana*.

(a) Suzuki (surname)

su zu ki

(b) fire

ka ji

(c) sign, indication

ki za shi

(d) family

ka zo ku

(e) scratch

ki zu

(f) Oze (place name)

o ze

(g) materials

so za i

(h) accident

ji ko

(i) cool

su zu shi i

4 Listen to your teacher or watch the Level 5 dictation video. Write the words in *hiragana* in the first squares as you hear them. Then, use the extra squares to practise writing the words again.

(a)

(b)

(c)

(d)

(e)

ISBN 9780170403948

Level 6: た to と

1 Practise writing the Level 6 *hiragana* in the squares. Use the dotted lines to help you balance your characters in the squares.

Hiragana	Memory aid	Stroke order
た **ta**	た **ta**	一 ナ ナ た
ち **chi**	ち **ch**eese ball	一 ち
つ **tsu**	つ a-**tsu**	つ
て **te**	て **te**nnis	て
と **to**	と **to**p	丶 と

6

ISBN 9780170403948

2 Read the *hiragana* in each leaf, and colour the leaves according to the key:

Key

ku ki (stem) – blue

ku sa (grass) – green

ku chi (mouth) – red

3 Highlight or circle the correct spelling for each word.

(a) **u chi** (home)
うさ
うち

(b) **o to** (sound)
おと
おつ

(c) **u tsu ku shi i** (beautiful)
うつしくい
うつくしい

(d) **o to ko** (man)
おとこ
あとこ

(e) **tsu i ta chi** (first of the month)
つこたち
ついたち

(f) **te ki** (enemy)
てき
とき

(g) **ta i ka i** (tournament)
たいかい
にいかい

(h) **tsu gi** (next)
つざ
つぎ

4 Onomatopoeia is when a word sounds like the thing it represents. Referring to the illustrations, write the Japanese onomatopoeic words in *hiragana*.

(a) prickly

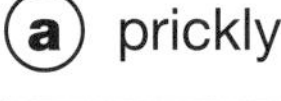

chi ku chi ku

(b) dozing off

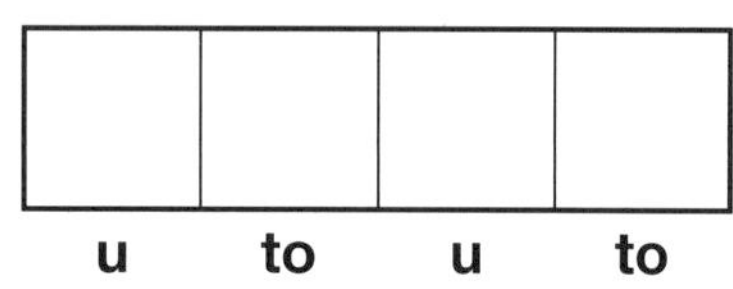

u to u to

(c) simmering

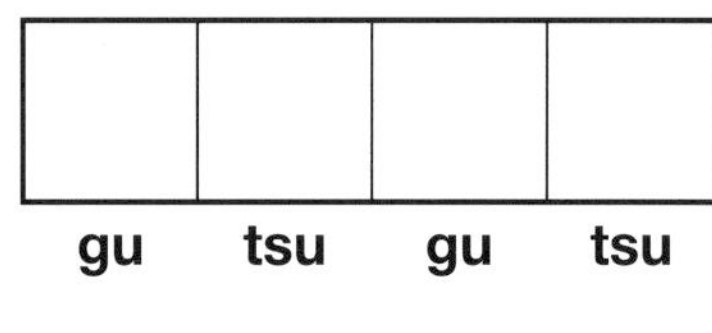

gu tsu gu tsu

(d) going a long way at a steady pace

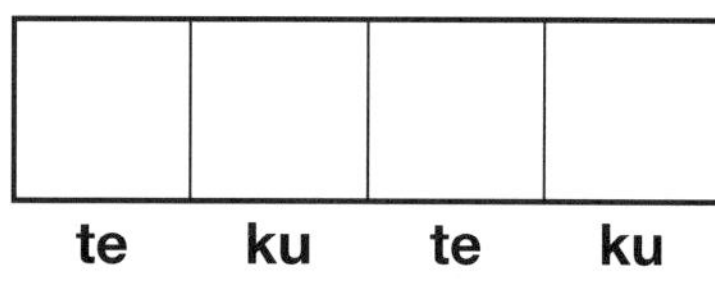

te ku te ku

ISBN 9780170403948

5 Write the words in *hiragana*.

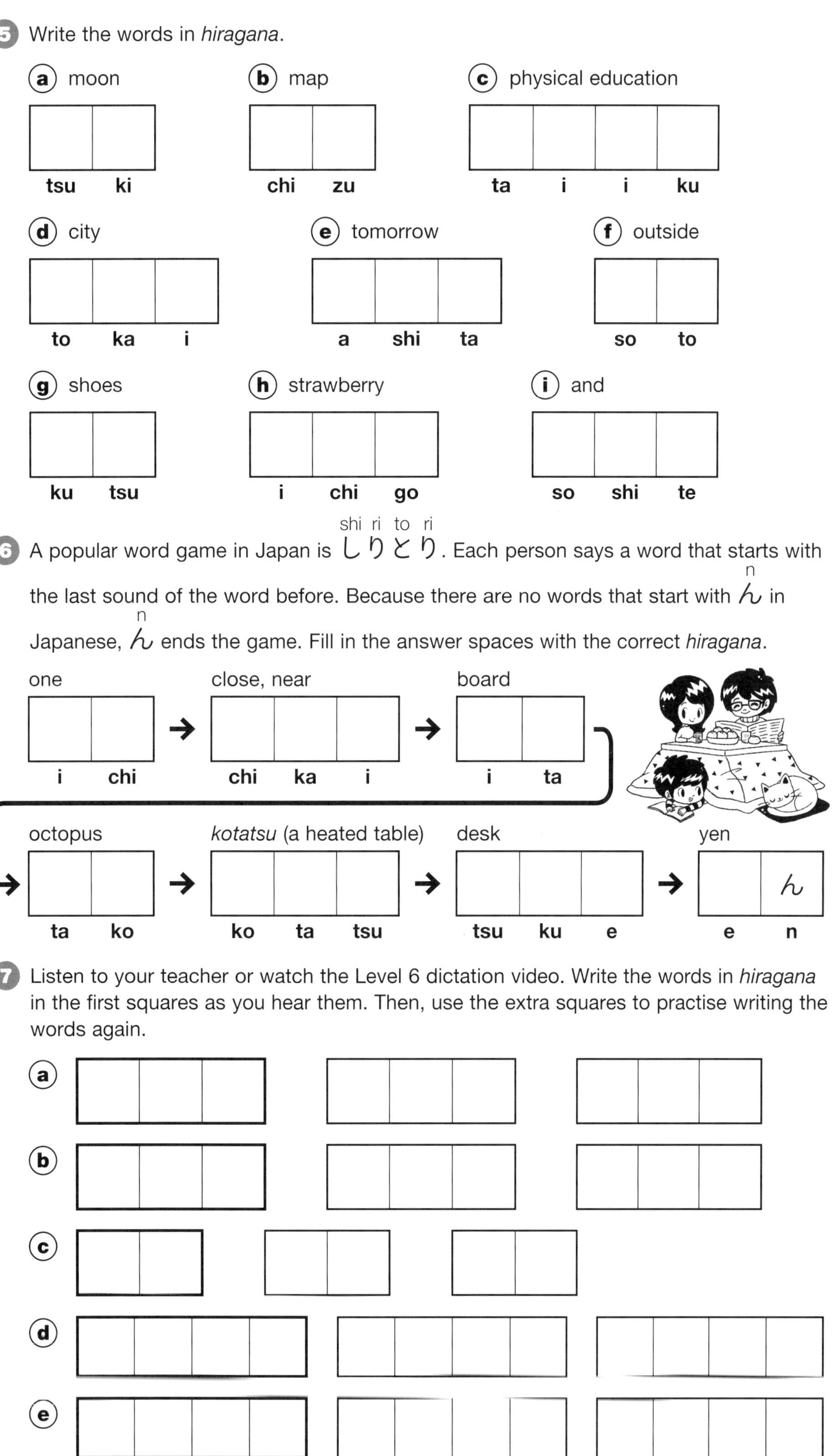

a) moon — tsu ki

b) map — chi zu

c) physical education — ta i i ku

d) city — to ka i

e) tomorrow — a shi ta

f) outside — so to

g) shoes — ku tsu

h) strawberry — i chi go

i) and — so shi te

6 A popular word game in Japan is しりとり (shi ri to ri). Each person says a word that starts with the last sound of the word before. Because there are no words that start with ん (n) in Japanese, ん (n) ends the game. Fill in the answer spaces with the correct *hiragana*.

one (i chi) → close, near (chi ka i) → board (i ta) → octopus (ta ko) → *kotatsu* (a heated table) (ko ta tsu) → desk (tsu ku e) → yen (e n) ん

7 Listen to your teacher or watch the Level 6 dictation video. Write the words in *hiragana* in the first squares as you hear them. Then, use the extra squares to practise writing the words again.

a)

b)

c)

d)

e)

6

ISBN 9780170403948

Level 7: だ to ど

1 Practise writing the Level 7 *hiragana* in the squares. Use the dotted lines to help you balance your characters in the squares.

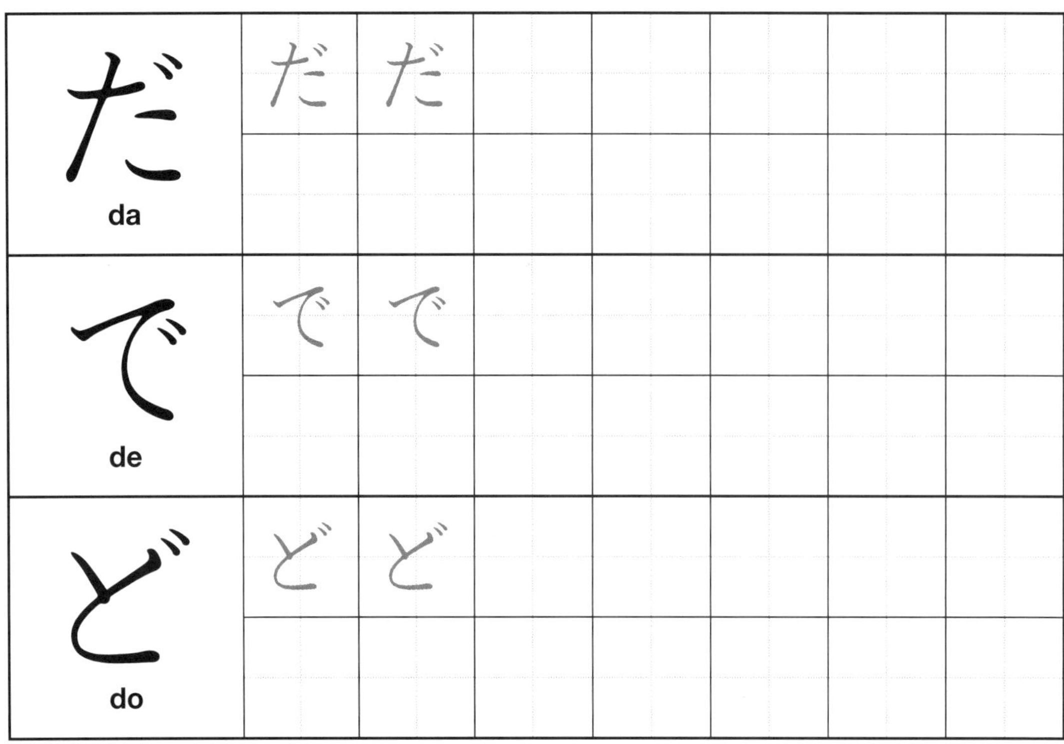

Adding ゛ to the upper-right of each *hiragana* in the *t* line makes a *d* sound. For example, *ta* becomes *da*, *te* becomes *de* and *to* becomes *do*.

To help you remember, think of **Te**d or **ta**da!

2 You have found three old letters, and you think they are instructions that lead to a treasure island (たからじま — ta ka ra ji ma). Choose a letter and follow the clues to see where you end up. Will 1, 2 or 3 take you to the treasure island?

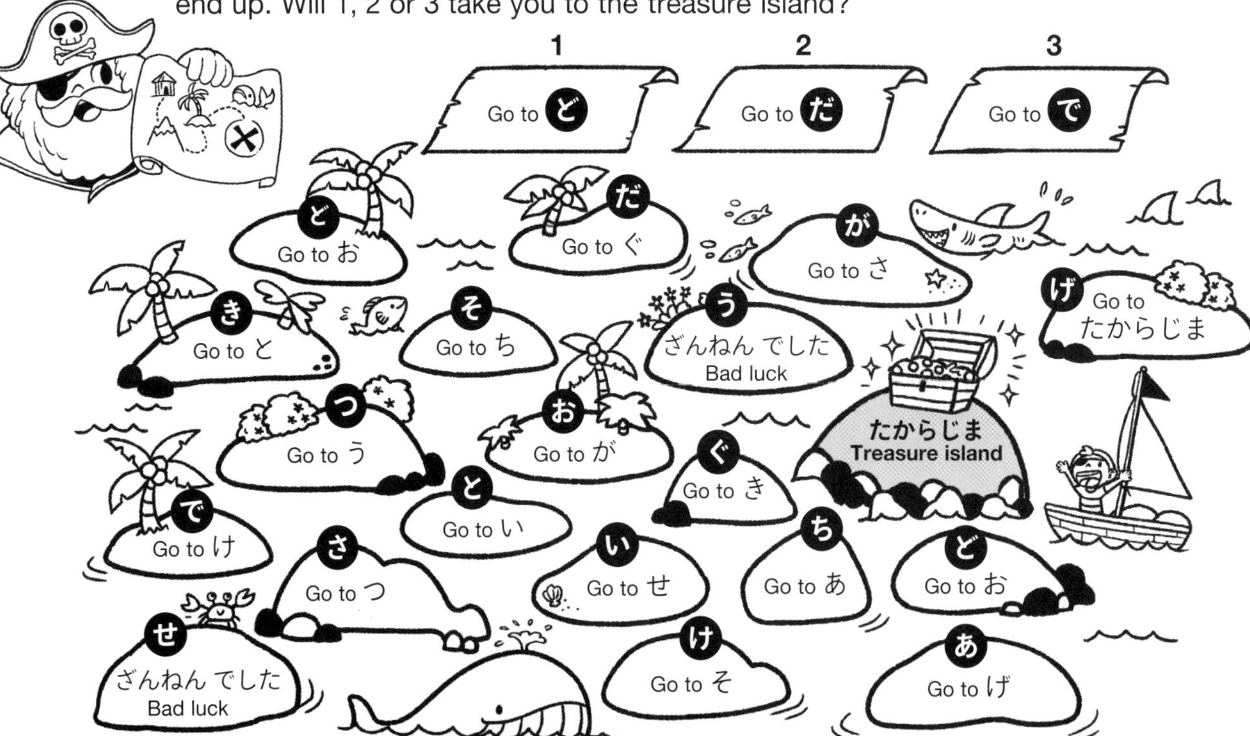

ISBN 9780170403948

3 Write the words in *hiragana*.

(a) soup stock

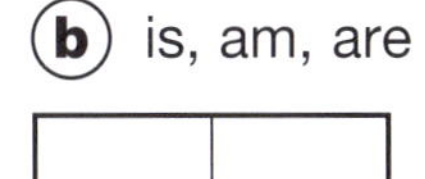

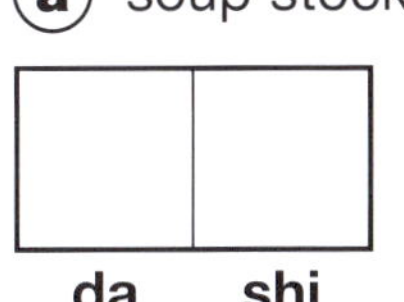

da shi

(b) is, am, are

de su

(c) sometimes

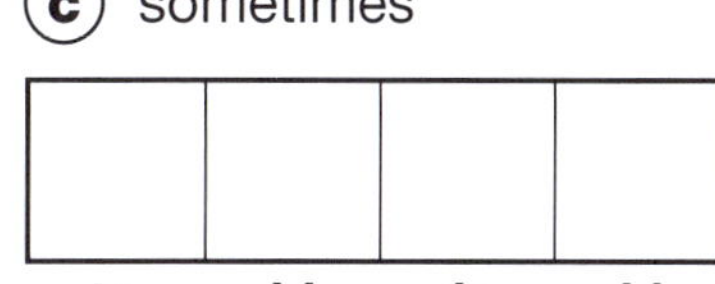

to ki do ki

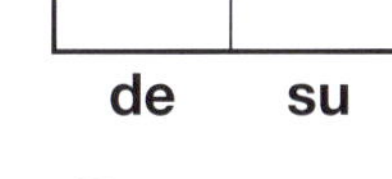

(d) sleeve

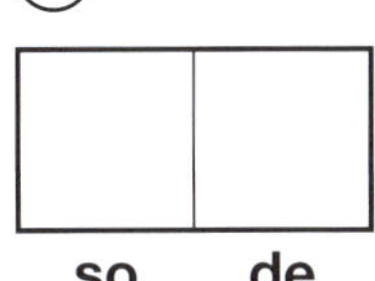

so de

(e) carpenter

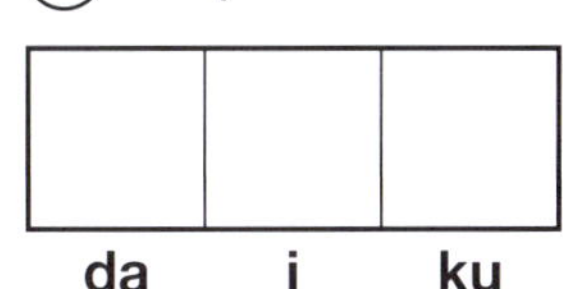

da i ku

(f) in a hurry

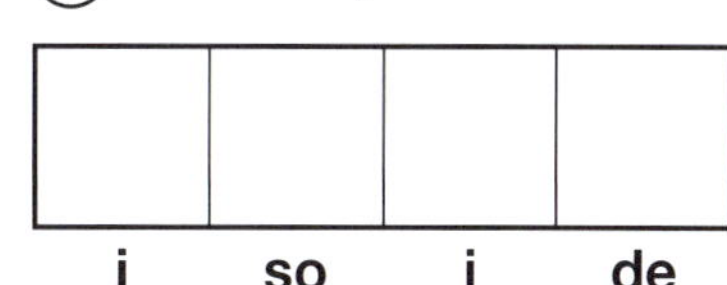

i so i de

(g) Edo Period

e do ji da i

(h) please

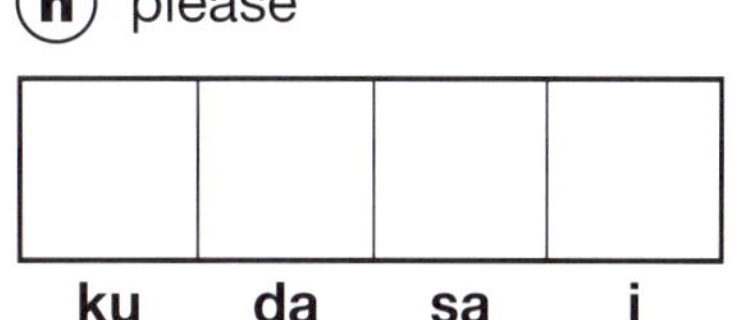

ku da sa i

4 Listen to your teacher or watch the Level 7 dictation video. Write the words in *hiragana* in the first squares as you hear them. Then, use the extra squares to practise writing the words again.

(a)

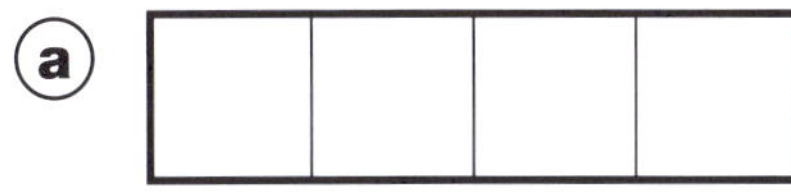
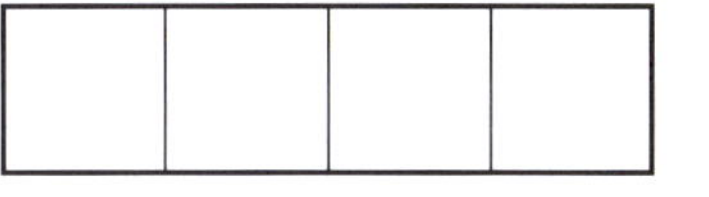
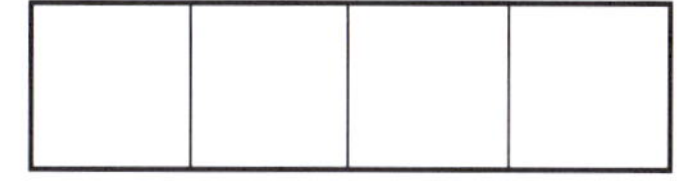

(b)

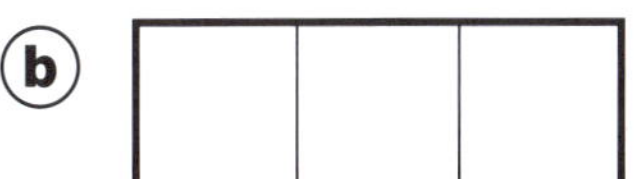
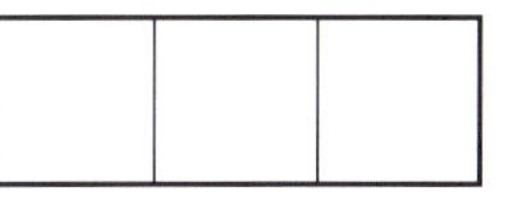
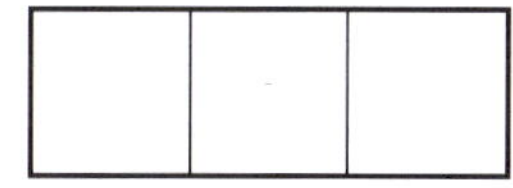

(c)

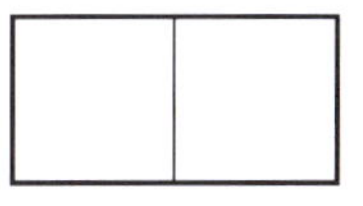

(d)

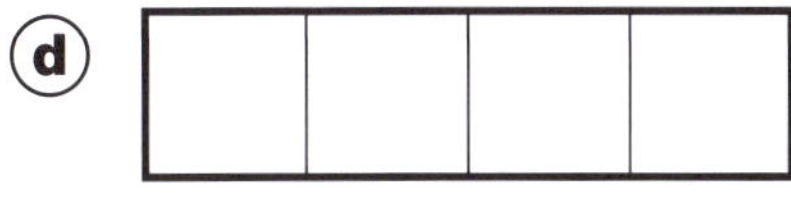
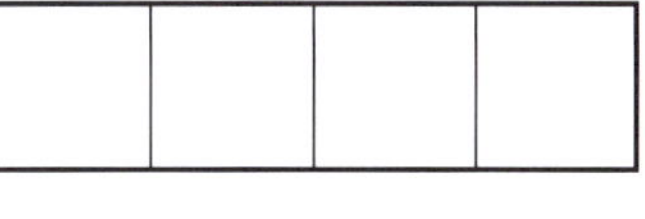
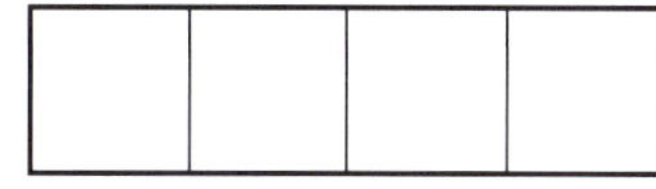

(e)

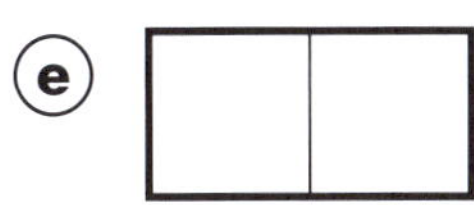
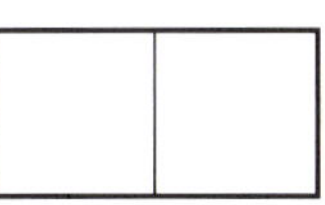
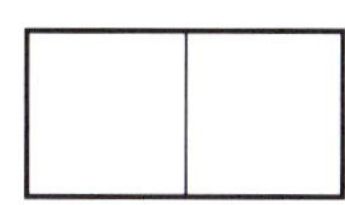

Were you wondering what happened to ち and つ? We only use *dakuten* with these two *hiragana* in special instances.

One such instance is when two words are joined together and the first part of the second word starts with ち or つ. For example:

- はな (ha na) (nose) + ち (chi) (blood) = はなぢ (ha na ji) (nosebleed)
- て (te) (hand) + つくり (tsu ku ri) (make) = てづくり (te zu ku ri) (handmade)

Here are some common words that use ぢ and づ:

- つづく (tsu zu ku) (continue)
- ちぢむ (chi ji mu) (shrink)
- おこづかい (o ko zu ka i) (pocket money)

Type 'di' for ぢ and 'du' for づ.

ISBN 9780170403948

Level 8: な to の

1 Practise writing the Level 8 *hiragana* in the squares. Use the dotted lines to help you balance your characters in the squares.

な na	な nun	一	ナ	ナ`	な		な
に ni	に knee	し	し一	に			
ぬ nu	ぬ noodle	ヽ	ぬ				
ね ne	ね net	丨	ね				
の no	の not	の					

ISBN 9780170403948

2 Cross out the extra *hiragana* to spell the words correctly.

a) **ne tsu** (fever) ねわつ

b) **na ga i** (long) なかがい

c) **no do** (throat) あのど

d) **ku ni** (country) そくに

e) **o na ka** (tummy) おなにか

f) **so no ta** (other) そのたに

g) **to ku ni** (especially) とくこに

h) **i ki nu ki** (relaxing activity) いきぬめき

8

3 Unjumble the *hiragana* to spell the words correctly.

a) **ki no ko** (mushroom) のきこ

b) **ni o i** (smell) おいに

c) **ko ne ko** (kitten) ねここ

d) **u na gi** (eel) ぎなう

e) **te nu gu i** (tea towel) ていぐぬ

4 Five words are hidden in the picture. Find them and work out their English meanings.

a) **na su** ____________

b) **ne gi** ____________

c) **i no shi shi** ____________

d) **ta nu ki** ____________

e) **tsu ki** ____________

Under the light of the moon, a raccoon watches as a wild boar eats an eggplant and a spring onion.

ISBN 9780170403948

5 Write the words in *hiragana*.

(a) my older brother

a ni

(b) cat

ne ko

(c) fish

sa ka na

(d) silk

ki nu

(e) my older sister

a ne

(f) fun

ta no shi i

(g) cloth

nu no

(h) bad at

ni ga te na

(i) summer

na tsu

6 Fill in each blank square of the *hiragana* sudoku so that each row (horizontal) and each column (vertical) includes な, に, ぬ, ね and の.

に	の	な		ぬ
		に	ぬ	な
ね	な		の	に
ぬ		ね		
	ぬ	の	に	ね

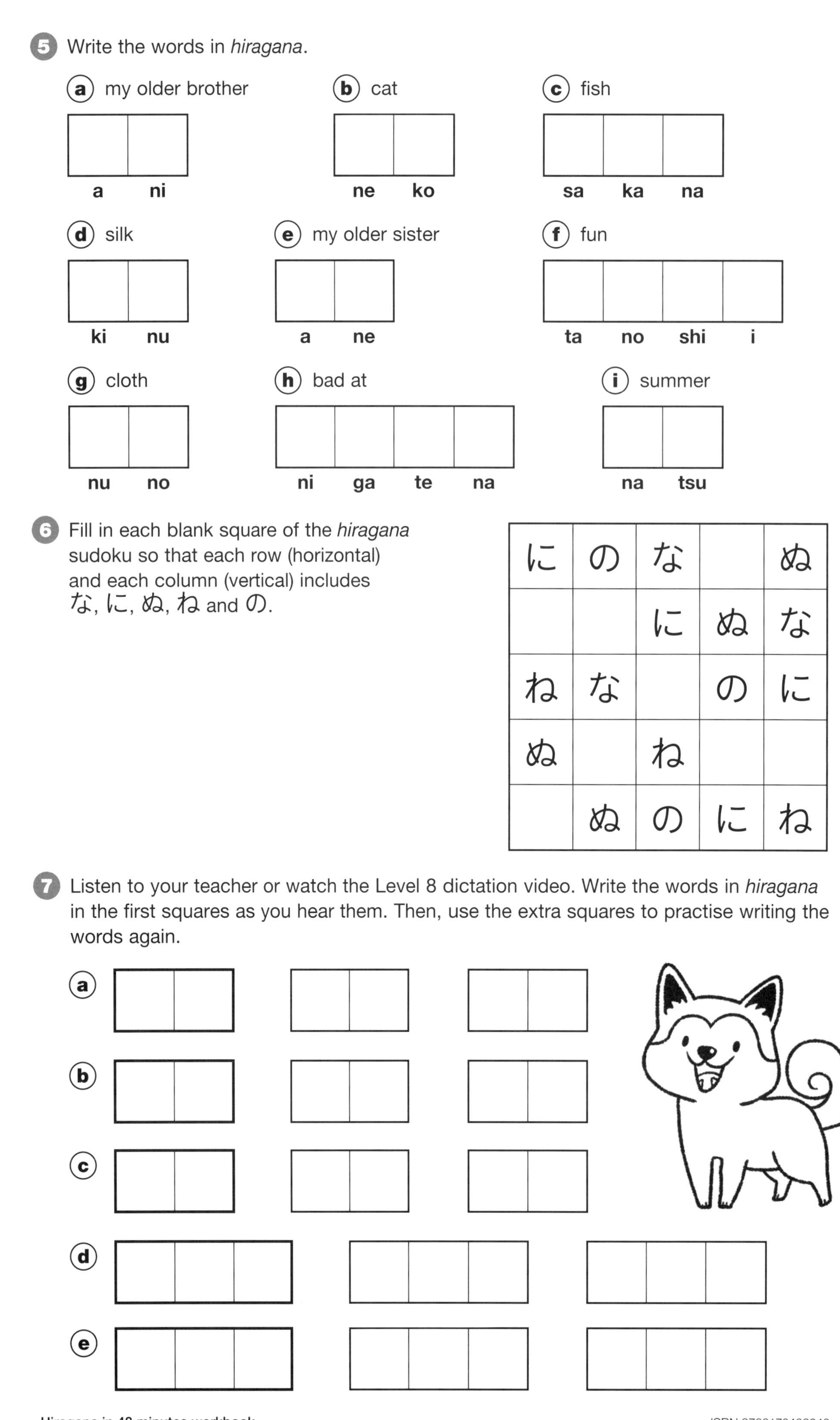

7 Listen to your teacher or watch the Level 8 dictation video. Write the words in *hiragana* in the first squares as you hear them. Then, use the extra squares to practise writing the words again.

(a)

(b)

(c)

(d)

(e)

ISBN 9780170403948

Level 9: は to ほ

1 Practise writing the Level 9 *hiragana* in the squares. Use the dotted lines to help you balance your characters in the squares.

Character	Mnemonic	Practice
は **ha**	は **ha** ha	は
ひ **hi**	ひ **hee** hee	ひ
ふ **fu**	ふ **Fu**ji-san	ふ
へ **he**	へ **hea**ven	へ
ほ **ho**	ほ **ho**t	ほ

9

ISBN 9780170403948

2 Colour the stars according to the key.

Key

ha shi (chopsticks) – green

ho shi (star) – yellow

ni shi (west) – red

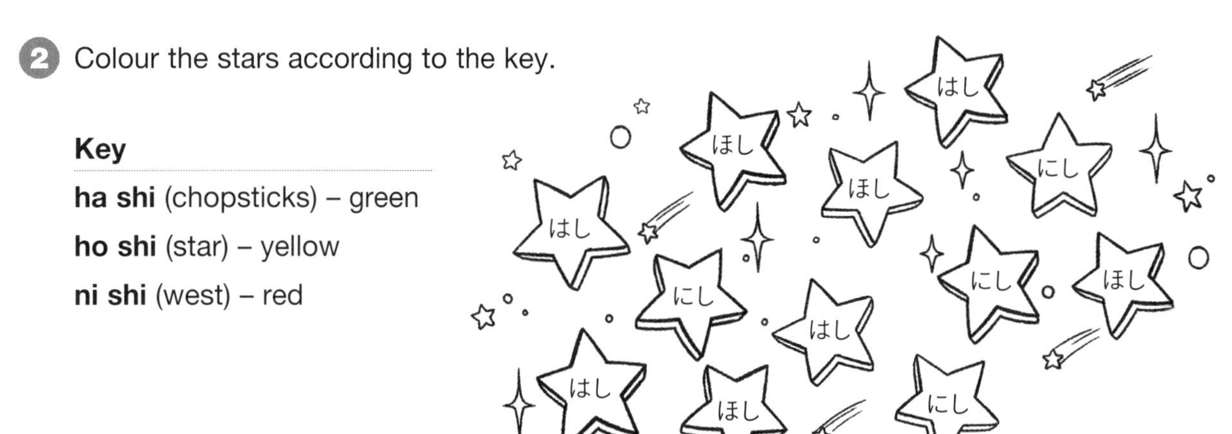

3 Draw lines connecting the letters from left to right to spell out the words pictured. The first one has been done for you.

a **fu ka i** (deep)

b **hi to tsu** (one thing)

c **he ki ga** (mural)

d **ho i ku** (childcare)

e **ha ta ke** (field for vegetables and fruit)

へ	き	け
ひ	か	が
ふ	い	い
は	た	く
ほ	と	つ

4 What is Naoko asking? Cross out every は, ひ, ふ, へ and ほ in the grid. Then, starting at the arrow at the top of the right-hand column, read down each column, moving from right to left. Write the eight remaining *hiragana* in the answer space to reveal Naoko's question.

				↓
す	ひ	す	ふ	ほ
ふ	で	ふ	へ	な
は	へ	は	が	ひ
か	ほ	き	へ	は
へ	は	ほ	は	つ

↓

								。

ISBN 9780170403948

5 Write the words in *hiragana*.

(a) star

ho shi

(b) belly button

he so

(c) clothes

fu ku

(d) sheep

hi tsu ji

(e) second of the month

fu tsu ka

(f) bone

ho ne

(g) my mother

ha ha

(h) person

hi to

(i) yes

ha i

6 A popular word game in Japan is しりとり (shi ri to ri). Each person says a word that starts with the last sound of the word before. Because there are no words that start with ん (n) in Japanese, ん (n) ends the game.

Use the rules of しりとり (shi ri to ri) to fill in the answer spaces with the words from the list.

- **tsu na hi ki** (tug of war game)
- **shi ha tsu** (first train)
- **a sa hi** (morning sun)
- **hi ki da shi** (drawer)
- **fu n** (minutes)
- **ki fu** (donation)

→ →

→ → ん

n

7 Listen to your teacher or watch the Level 9 dictation video. Write the words in *hiragana* in the first squares as you hear them. Then, use the extra squares to practise writing the words again.

(a)

(b)

(c)

(d)

(e)

9

ISBN 9780170403948

Level 10: ば to ぽ

1. Practise writing the Level 10 *hiragana* in the squares. Use the dotted lines to help you balance your characters in the squares.

ば	ba	ば	ば						
び	bi	び	び						
ぶ	bu	ぶ	ぶ						ぶ
べ	be	べ	べ						
ぼ	bo	ぼ	ぼ						

Adding the symbol ゛ to the upper-right of *hiragana* in the h line makes a b sound. For example, *ha* becomes *ba*, and *he* becomes *be*.

To help you remember, think of **h**ub or **h**uman **b**eing.

ぱ	pa	ぱ	ぱ						
ぴ	pi	ぴ	ぴ						
ぷ	pu	ぷ	ぷ						ぷ
ぺ	pe	ぺ	ぺ						
ぽ	po	ぽ	ぽ						

Adding ° to *hiragana* on the h line makes p sounds. For example, *ha* becomes *pa*, and *he* becomes *pe*.

To help you remember, think of **h**o**p** or **h**a**pp**y.

The formal name of this symbol is *han-dakuten*, but it is also commonly known as *maru*.

ISBN 9780170403948

2 Find these words in the word search puzzle. You will find them in every direction, including diagonally and backwards.

a **pa ku pa ku** ______________ eating heartily

b **pi ka pi ka** ______________ shining, glittery

c **pu chi pu chi** ______________ popping noise

d **pe ko pe ko** ______________ very hungry

e **po ta po ta** ______________ dripping water

ぽ	ぱ	こ	ぺ	こ	ぺ	こ
ぱ	た	ぴ	か	ぴ	く	ぴ
く	か	ぽ	ぺ	ぱ	か	ぱ
ぽ	ぴ	こ	た	く	ぴ	ぴ
ち	ぷ	ち	ぷ	ぱ	か	ぽ
ぽ	た	ぷ	ち	く	ぴ	ぺ

3 Find the spelling errors and rewrite the words correctly in *hiragana*.

a **ki bi shi i** (strict)

さ ひ し い

b **ka bi** (mould)

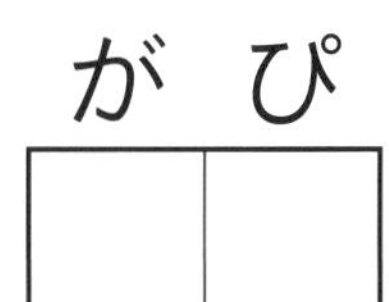

c **fu de ba ko** (pencil case)

d **a bu na i** (dangerous)

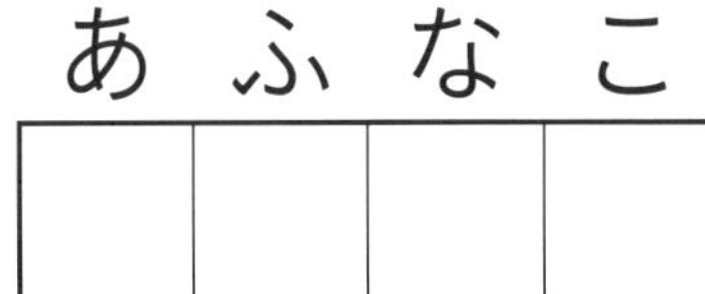

e **ha na bi** (fireworks)

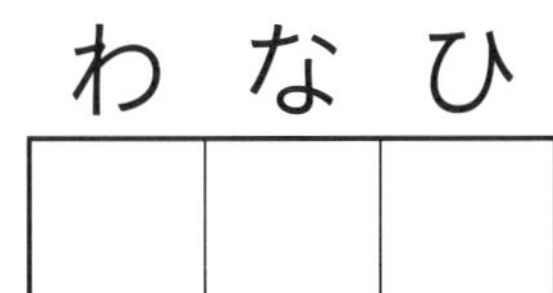

f **ka bu to** (warrior helmet)

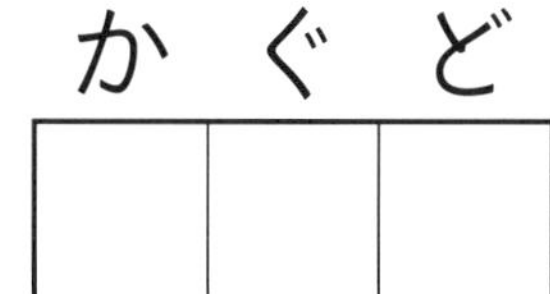

g **ka ba** (hippo)

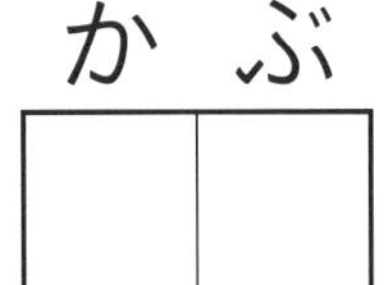

h **na be** (pot)

i **so bo** (my grandmother)

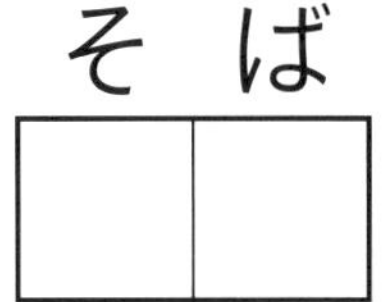

j **sa n po** (a walk)

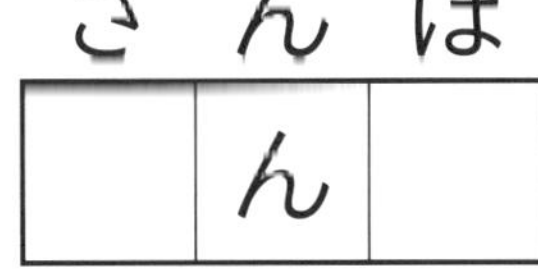

k **shi n pa i** (worry)

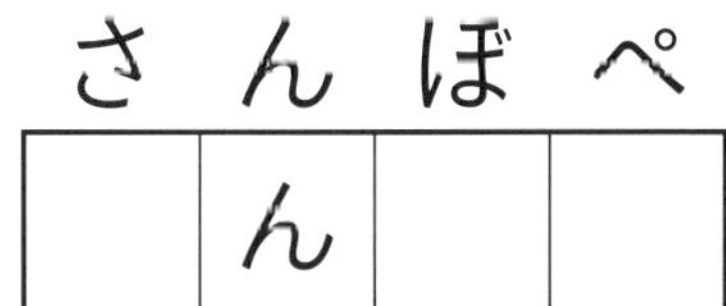

10

ISBN 9780170403948

4 Write the words in *hiragana*.

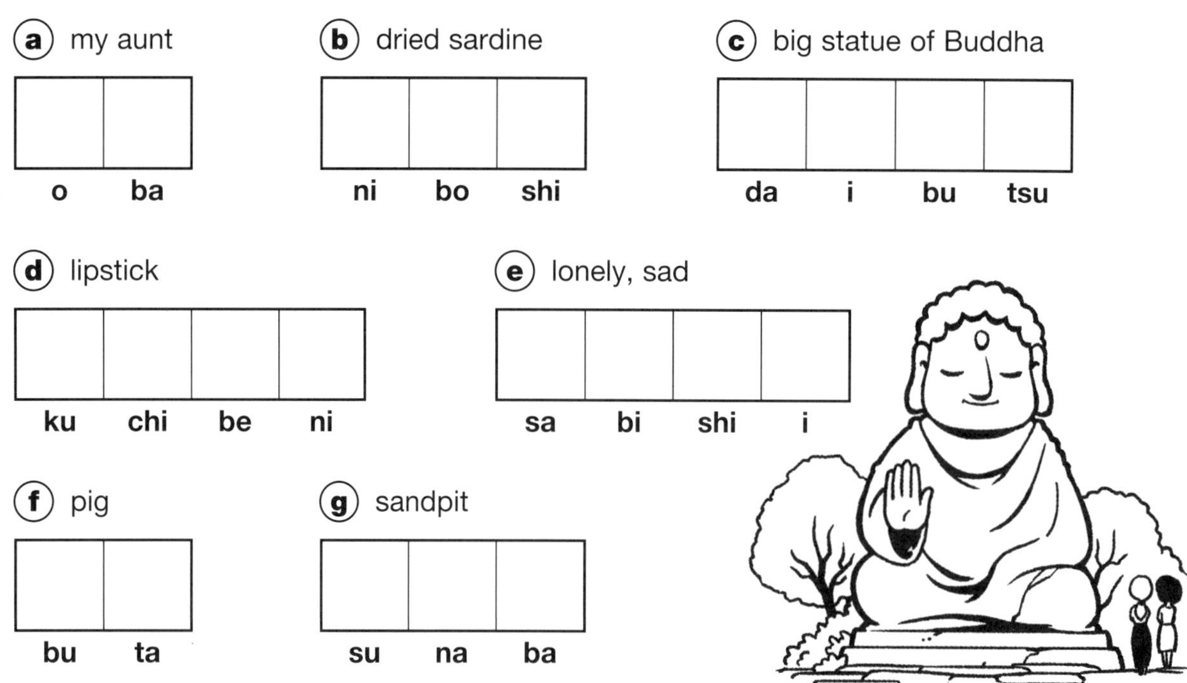

(a) my aunt — o ba

(b) dried sardine — ni bo shi

(c) big statue of Buddha — da i bu tsu

(d) lipstick — ku chi be ni

(e) lonely, sad — sa bi shi i

(f) pig — bu ta

(g) sandpit — su na ba

5 Listen to your teacher or watch the Level 10 dictation video. Write the words in *hiragana* in the first squares as you hear them. Then, use the extra squares to practise writing the words again.

(a)

(b)

(c)

(d)

(e)

(f)

(g)

ISBN 9780170403948

Level 11: ま to よ

1. Practise writing the Level 11 *hiragana* in the squares. Use the dotted lines to help you balance your characters in the squares.

ま ma	ま mum	一	二	ま			
み mi	み me	み	み				
む mu	む moo	一	む	む			む
め me	め mess	㇐	め				
も mo	も more	し	も	も			も

11

ISBN 9780170403948

や **ya**	 や **ya**rd			や			や
ゆ **yu**	 ゆ **u**-turn		ゆ				ゆ
よ **yo**	よ **yo**yo		よ				

2 Use coloured pens or pencils to colour in the matching pairs.

ISBN 9780170403948

3 Complete each *hiragana* by adding the missing stroke.

4 Find a path through the maze by following the correct *hiragana* spellings of the four phrases.

- **ta no shi i o mo i de** (fun memories)
- **o i shi i sa shi mi** (delicious sashimi)
- **ya su i mi se** (cheap shop)
- **ni gi ya ka na ma chi** (bustling town)

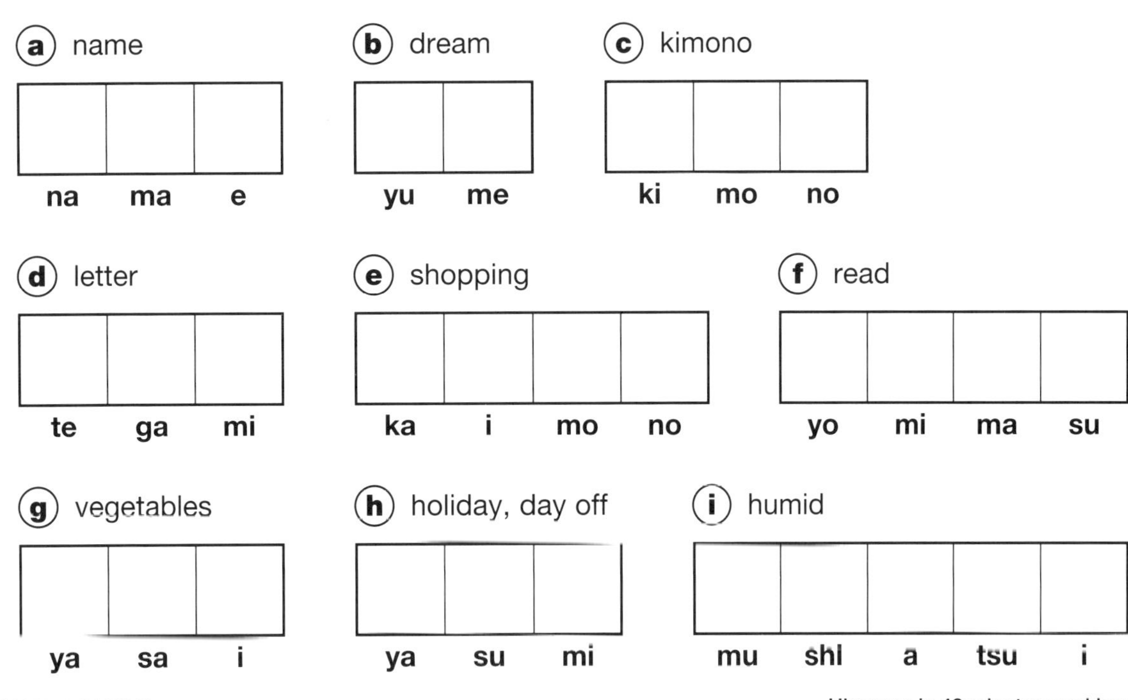

5 Write the words in *hiragana*.

(a) name

na ma e

(b) dream

yu me

(c) kimono

ki mo no

(d) letter

te ga mi

(e) shopping

ka i mo no

(f) read

yo mi ma su

(g) vegetables

ya sa i

(h) holiday, day off

ya su mi

(i) humid

mu shi a tsu i

ISBN 9780170403948

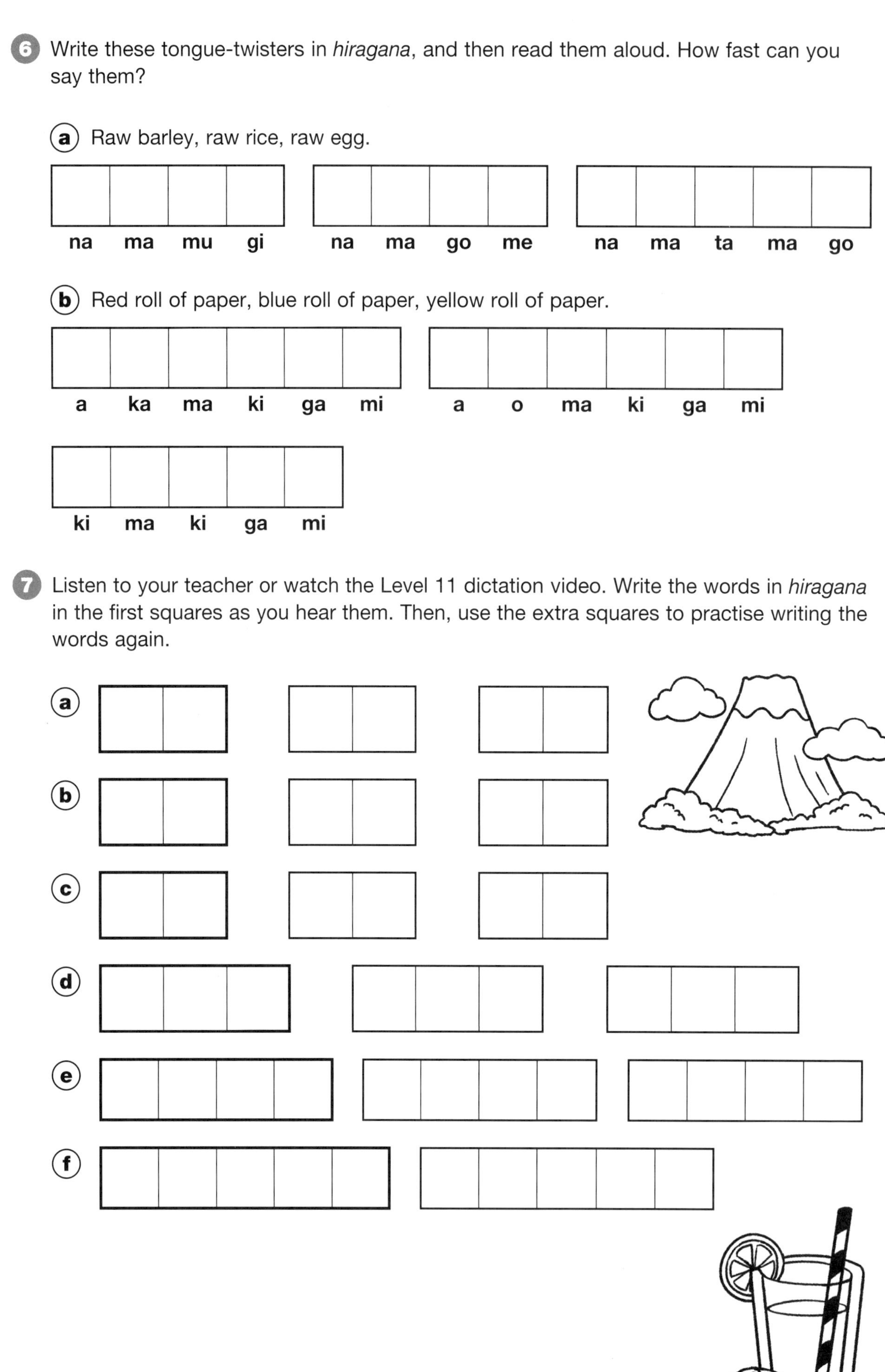

6 Write these tongue-twisters in *hiragana*, and then read them aloud. How fast can you say them?

(a) Raw barley, raw rice, raw egg.

na	ma	mu	gi

na	ma	go	me

na	ma	ta	ma	go

(b) Red roll of paper, blue roll of paper, yellow roll of paper.

a	ka	ma	ki	ga	mi

a	o	ma	ki	ga	mi

ki	ma	ki	ga	mi

7 Listen to your teacher or watch the Level 11 dictation video. Write the words in *hiragana* in the first squares as you hear them. Then, use the extra squares to practise writing the words again.

(a)

(b)

(c)

(d)

(e)

(f)

ISBN 9780170403948

Level 12: ら to ん

1. Practise writing the Level 12 *hiragana* in the squares. Use the dotted lines to help you balance your characters in the squares.

Hiragana	Mnemonic	Practice
ら ra	**ru**n	ら
り ri	**ri**ver	り
る ru	**ru**by	る
れ re	**re**d squirrel	れ
ろ ro	**ro**bber	ろ

12

ISBN 9780170403948

わ **wa**	 わ **wo**nderful	｜	わ				
を **o**	 を **O**lympic	一		を			
ん **n**	 ん e**n**d	ん					

There are two *o* sounds in the *hiragana* chart. One, お is used to write words, and the other, を, is a particle. To help tell them apart, the *romaji* for お is *o* and the *romaji* for を is *wo*. However, you should always pronounce を as 'o' just the same as お.

Japanese punctuation marks are different from English punctuation marks. Look at the examples of a Japanese full stop and a comma.

full stop 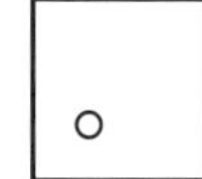

comma 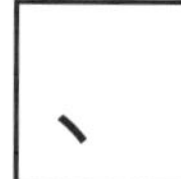

You should write Japanese punctuation marks in the lower-left of the squares in Japanese writing paper and answer squares.

2 Find the words in the text, and highlight or colour them appropriately.

だいすき (love) .... blue

おんがく (music) .... red

からて (karate) .... green

わたし は まいにち おんがく を
ききます。すきな おんがく は
Jポップ です。でも、がっき が
できません。スポーツ が だいすき
です。すいようび に からて の
れんしゅう を します。わたし は
からて が とくい です。

ISBN 9780170403948

3 Find two mistakes in each sentence. Circle the errors. Then, rewrite the sentences correctly.

ⓐ **fu ru i o te ra ga a ri ma su.** (There is an old temple.)

ⓑ **hi ru go ha n wo tsu ku ri ma su.** (I make lunch.)

4 Write the words in *hiragana*.

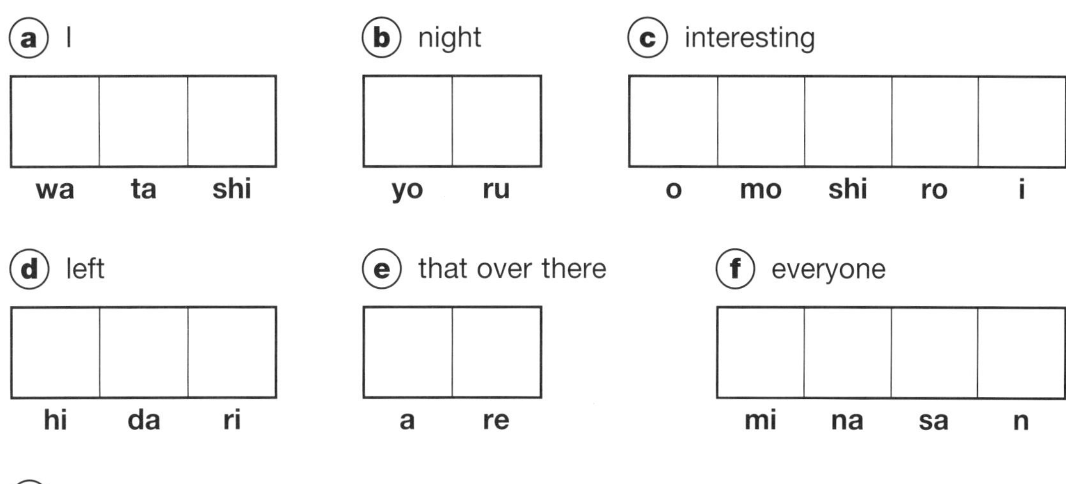

ⓖ I read comics.

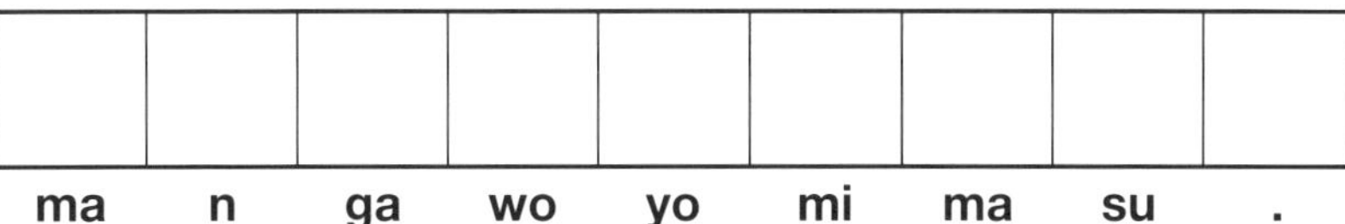

5 Write the Japanese word jokes in *hiragana*.

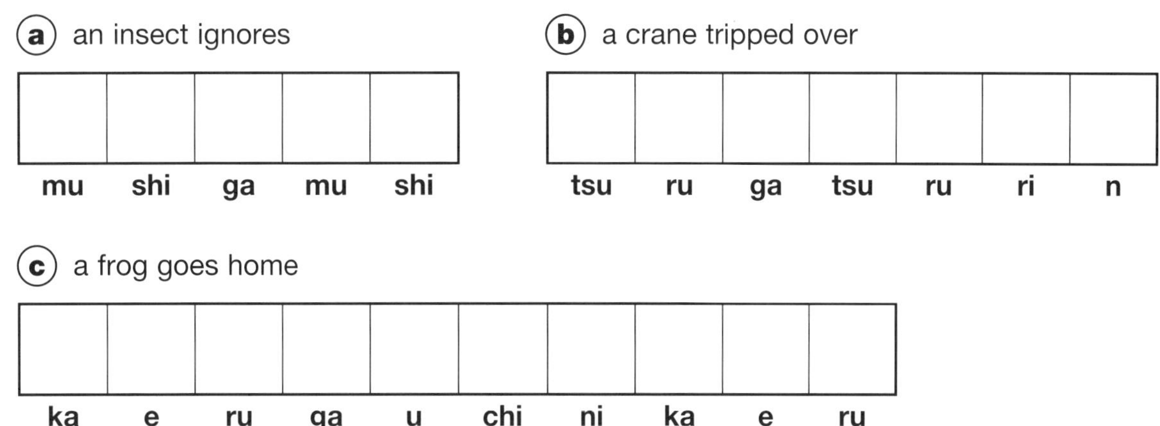

12

ISBN 9780170403948

6 Which door leads to the exit? Choose a door (1–3) and follow the instructions to see where you end up. If you do not reach the exit, try another door.

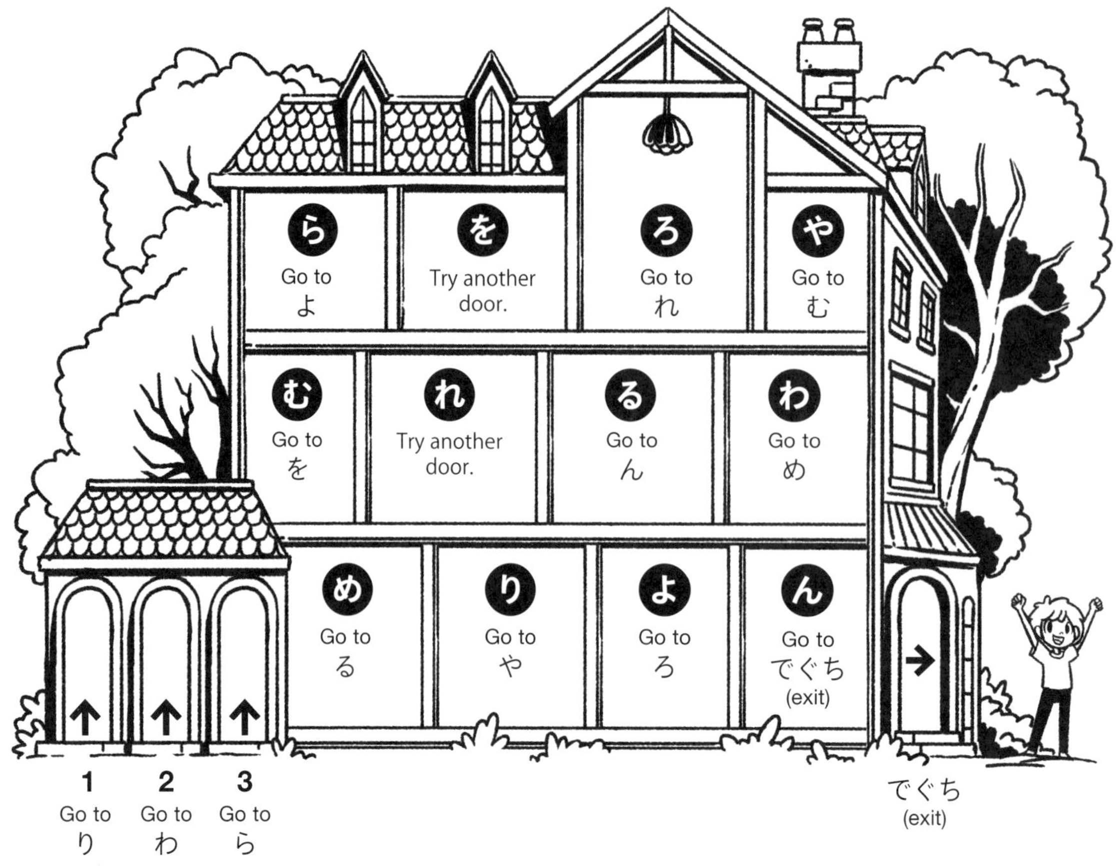

7 Listen to your teacher or watch the Level 12 dictation video. Write the words in *hiragana* in the first squares as you hear them. Then, use the extra squares to practise writing the words again.

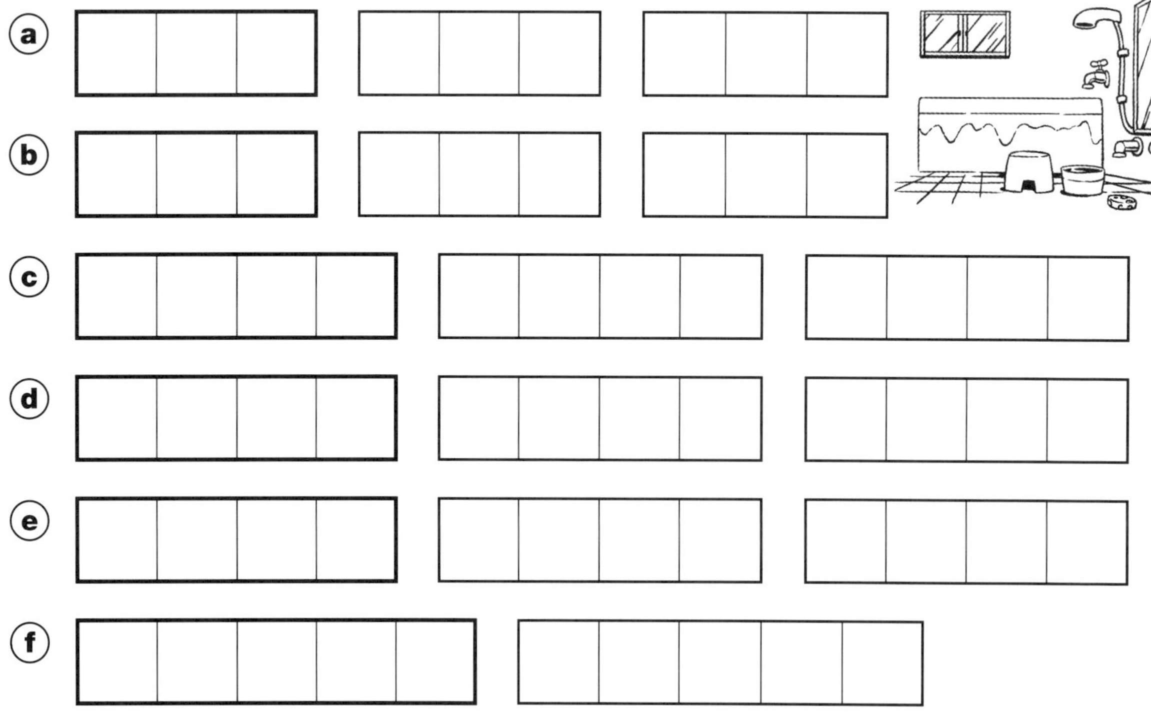

Congratulations! You have learnt all 46 *hiragana*.

ISBN 9780170403948

Level 13: Similar *hiragana*

Let's practise similar *hiragana*.

Set 1

Set 1
i い
ko こ
ri り

1 Circle or highlight the correct spelling of each word.

a **ho ko ri** (pride)

はこり
ほりこ
ほこい
ほこり

b **ko i shi** (pebbles)

いしこ
しこい
こいし
いこし

c **ma tsu ri** (festival)

まつこ
まつり
まつい
まこり

2 Fill in the blanks to complete the words.

a chair

[ ] す
i

b a little

す [ ] し
ko

c origami paper

お [ ] がみ
ri

Set 2

Set 2
ra ら
ru る
ro ろ

3 Each word has one or more incorrect *hiragana*. Rewrite the word correctly.

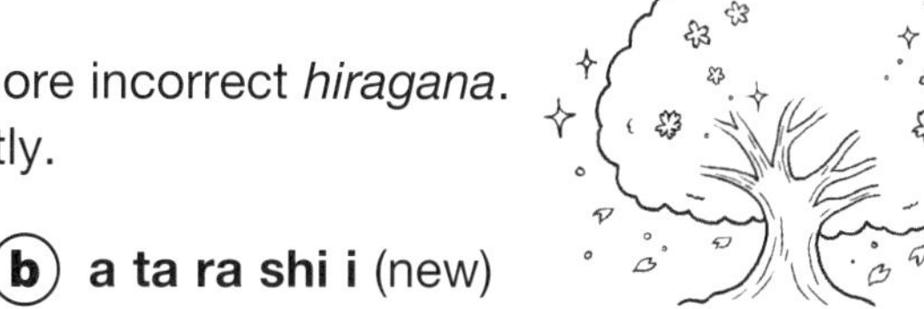

a **to ko ro** (place)

と い る

b **a ta ra shi i** (new)

あ た ろ し い

c **hi ru** (daytime)

ひ ら

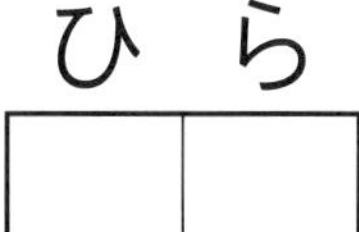

d **ku ru ma** (car)

く ろ ま

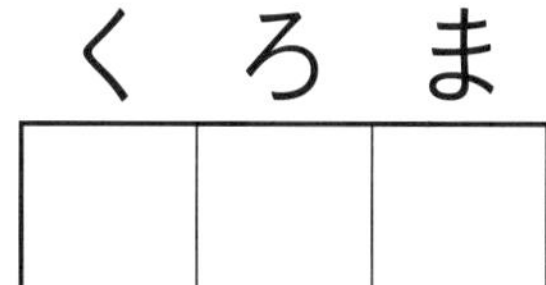

e **ku ro** (black)

く る

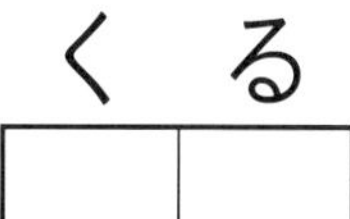

f **sa ku ra** (cherry blossom)

き く る

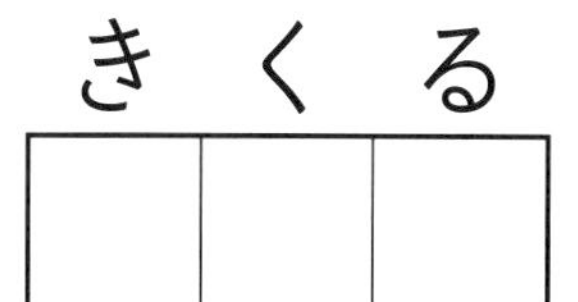

g **o fu ro** (bath)

あ ふ る

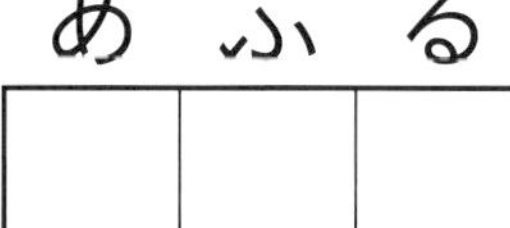

h **a ka ru i** (cheerful)

あ か ら り

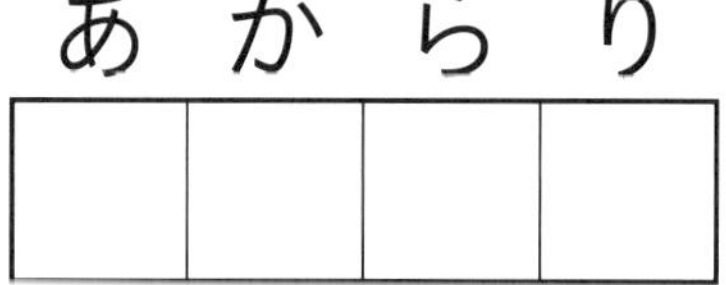

i **shi ro** (white)

し る

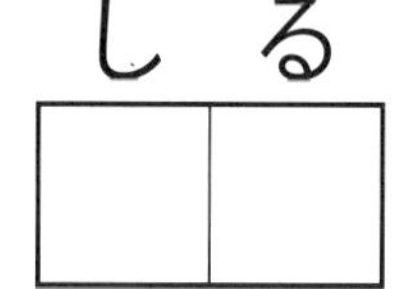

13

ISBN 9780170403948

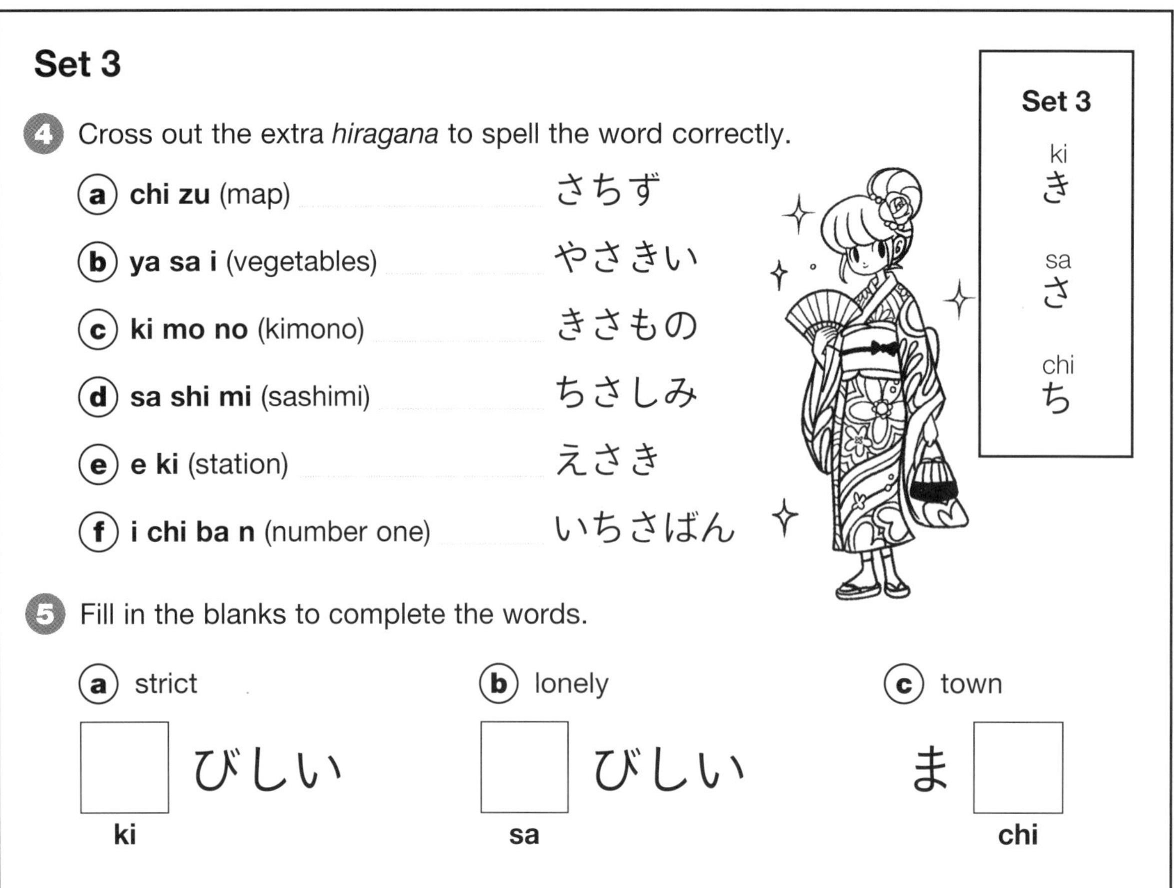

Set 3

4 Cross out the extra *hiragana* to spell the word correctly.

ⓐ **chi zu** (map) ……… さちず

ⓑ **ya sa i** (vegetables) ……… やさきい

ⓒ **ki mo no** (kimono) ……… きさもの

ⓓ **sa shi mi** (sashimi) ……… ちさしみ

ⓔ **e ki** (station) ……… えさき

ⓕ **i chi ba n** (number one) ……… いちさばん

Set 3
ki き
sa さ
chi ち

5 Fill in the blanks to complete the words.

ⓐ strict	ⓑ lonely	ⓒ town
□びしい	□びしい	ま□
ki	**sa**	**chi**

Set 4

6 Connect the *romaji* and definitions to their *hiragana* equivalents.

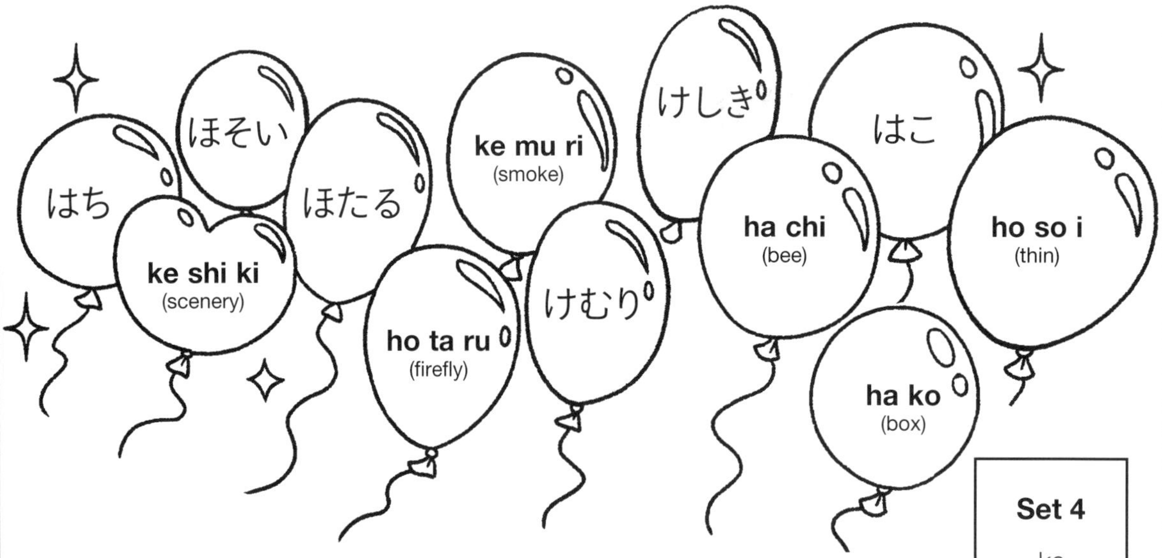

はち

ほそい

ほたる

けしき

はこ

けむり

ke shi ki (scenery)

ke mu ri (smoke)

ho ta ru (firefly)

ha chi (bee)

ho so i (thin)

ha ko (box)

7 Fill in the blanks to complete the words.

ⓐ field (for vegetables and fruit)	ⓑ caterpillar	ⓒ book
□たけ	□むし	□ん
ha	**ke**	**ho**

Set 4
ke け
ha は
ho ほ

ISBN 9780170403948

Set 5

8 Draw lines connecting the letters from left to right to spell out the words pictured.

Set 5
ne ね
re れ
wa わ

ⓐ  **o ka ne** (money) お い し

ⓑ **ka i wa** (conversation) れ か わ

ⓒ  **re ki shi** (history) か き ね

9 Fill in the blanks to complete the words.

ⓐ pyjamas
□ まき
ne

ⓑ scary
こ □ い
wa

ⓒ violet (flower)
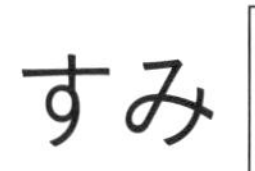
すみ □
re

Set 6

10 Choose the correct *hiragana* from the brackets to complete each word.

ⓐ **a o** (blue) .... (あ, ぬ, め) お

ⓑ **i nu** (dog) .... い (あ, ぬ, め)

ⓒ **yu me** (dream) .... ゆ (あ, ぬ, め)

ⓓ **nu i gu ru mi** (soft toy) .... (あ, ぬ, め) いぐるみ

ⓔ **a shi** (leg, foot) .... (あ, ぬ, め) し

ⓕ **tsu me** (finger nail) .... つ (あ, ぬ, め)

Set 6
a あ
nu ぬ
me め

11 Fill in the blanks to complete the words.

ⓐ glasses
□ がね
me

ⓑ raccoon

た □ き
nu

ⓒ rain
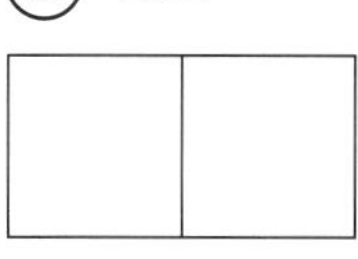
□ □
a me

13

ISBN 9780170403948

Level 14: Vertical writing 1

Traditionally, Japanese was only written vertically. These days, however, Japanese is written vertically and horizontally.

Tanzaku たんざく

1 Let's practise writing vertically by copying some たんざく. Every year at the Star Festival, たなばた, on 7 July, people write their wishes onto たんざく. They hang the たんざく on bamboo branches and pray for their wishes to be granted.

To write vertically in Japanese, start at the top right-hand square and move down the first column. Continue at the top of the next column.

Notice that the full stop and comma are written in the top-right corner of a square when you write vertically.

Copy the たんざく messages in the empty squares. Usually, たんざく do not have writing squares, but squares are provided here as a helpful guide.

いぬが、かいたいです。

(I want a dog.)

おきなわに、いきたいです。

(I want to go to Okinawa.)

Class activity

It is bingo time! Write any nine words, each starting with different *hiragana*. Then, listen to your teacher read out Japanese words. If a word said by your teacher starts with a *hiragana* that matches the first *hiragana* of any of your words, cross out the word. The first student to cross out any three words in a row (horizontally, vertically or diagonally) is the winner. やった!

ISBN 9780170403948

Level 15: Long vowels

Japanese speakers use long vowel sounds and short vowel sounds, and the difference between them is very important. Changing how you say a vowel can change the meaning of a word.

Let's study how to write long vowel sounds in *hiragana*.

A sounds

Write あ after the sound that needs to be long.

- おかあさん (mother) – pronounce the **ka** sound long
  o **ka** → sa n
- おばあさん (grandmother) – pronounce the **ba** sound long
  o **ba** → sa n

I sounds

Write い after the sound that needs to be long.

- おにいさん (older brother) – pronounce the **ni** sound long
  o **ni** → sa n
- しいたけ (shiitake mushroom) – pronounce the **shi** sound long
  shi → ta ke

U sounds

Write う after the sound that needs to be long.

- すうがく (mathematics) – pronounce the **su** sound long
  su → ga ku
- くうき (air) – pronounce the **ku** sound long
  ku → ki

E sounds

Write い after the sound that needs to be long, even though it is an *e* sound.

- えいご (English) – pronounce the **e** sound long
  e → go
- けいたい (mobile phone) – pronounce the **ke** sound long
  ke → ta i

An exception is おねえさん (older sister)
o **ne** → sa n

O sounds

Write う after the sound that needs to be long, even though it is an *o* sound.

- いもうと (my younger sister) – pronounce the **mo** sound long
  i **mo** → to
- とうふ (tofu) – pronounce the **to** sound long
  to → fu

There are a few special words that use お to show a long *o* sound.

- おおきい (big)
  o → ki i
- とおい (far)
  to → i
- おおい (many)
  o → i
- とおか (10th of the month)
  to → ka

ISBN 9780170403948

1 Read the words aloud, paying attention to the long vowels.

a おばさん (aunt) おばあさん (grandmother)

b おじさん (uncle) おじいさん (grandfather)

c ゆめ (dream) ゆうめい (famous)

d いえ (house) いいえ (no)

2 Choose the correct spelling of each word.

a **a ri ga to➔** (thank you)

ありがと
ありがとう
ありがとお

b **ka te➔ ka** (home economics)

かてえか
かてか
かていか

c **o ka➔ sa n** (mother)

おかあさん
おかさん
おかえさん

d **chi➔ sa i** (small)

ちさい
ちいさい
ちえさい

e **ho➔ ka go** (after school)

ほおかご
ほうかご
ほかご

f **o➔ i** (many)

おうい
おい
おおい

3 Find three words with long vowels in the text, and rewrite them in the squares.

わたし は どようび に ともだち と
こうえん に いきました。それから、
おもしろい えいが を みました。
たのしかった です。

ISBN 9780170403948

We have used arrows to help you understand where the long vowels are. Now, we will give *romaji* hints to help you write long vowel sounds correctly in *hiragana*.

4 Write the words in *hiragana*.

ⓐ goodbye

sa yo u na ra

ⓑ older sister

o ne e sa n

ⓒ far

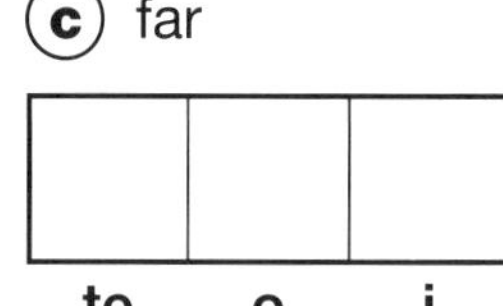

to o i

5 Complete the crossword puzzle in *hiragana*.

Across

2 **o o ki i** (big)
4 **bu do u** (grapes)
5 **ko u e n** (park)
7 **bo u shi** (hat, cap)
8 **to ke i** (clock)
9 **zo u** (elephant)

Down

1 **ko u ko u** (high school)
3 **o be n to u** (packed lunch)
6 **u shi** (cow)

6 Listen to your teacher or watch the Level 15 dictation video.
Write the words in *hiragana* in the first squares as you hear them.
Then, use the extra squares to practise writing the words again.

ⓐ
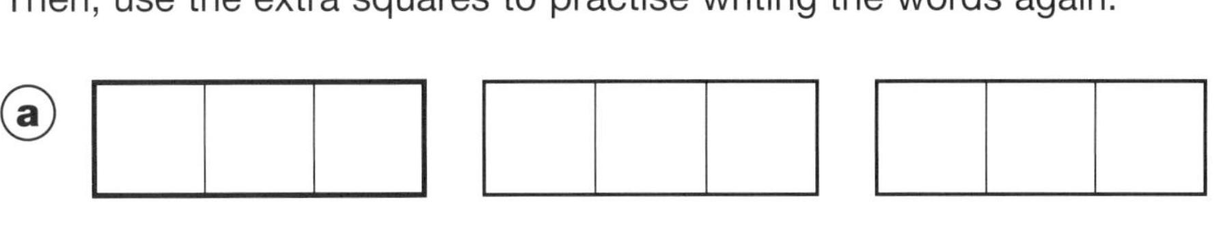

ⓑ
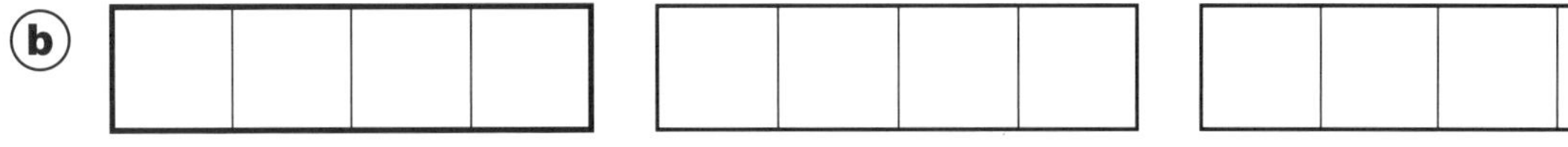

ⓒ
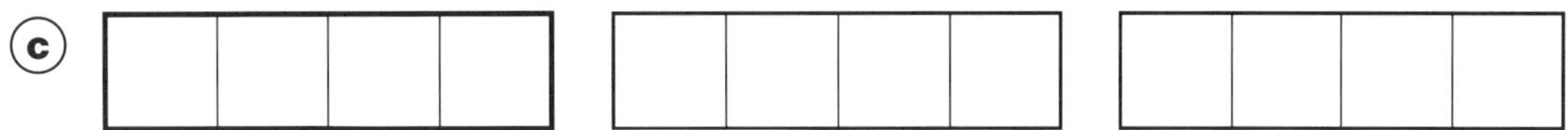

ⓓ
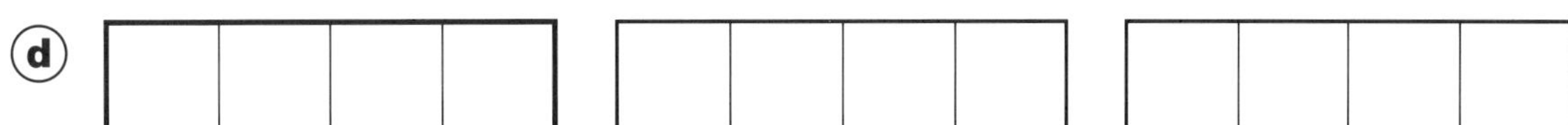

ⓔ

ⓕ
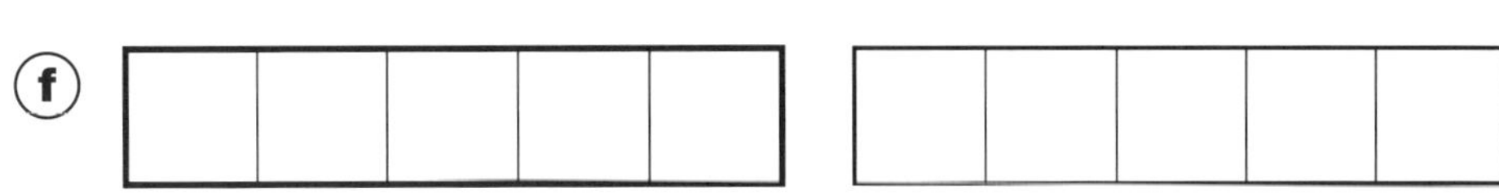

15

ISBN 9780170403948

Level 16: Combination sounds

Japanese people use *hiragana* to write combination sounds or *youon*. These sounds are written by writing a full-size *i*-sound *hiragana* with a smaller や, ゆ or よ.

- shi ya sha
し + small や = しゃ
- gi yu gyu
ぎ + small ゆ = ぎゅ
- chi yo cho
ち + small よ = ちょ

Although there are two characters, they are pronounced together as one sound or syllable. When written, the small や, ゆ and よ are about one-quarter of the size of normal *hiragana* and are written in the lower-left of each square.

1 Practise writing combination sounds.

きゃ	kya	きゃ	
きゅ	kyu	きゅ	
きょ	kyo	きょ	
しゃ	sha	しゃ	
しゅ	shu	しゅ	
しょ	sho	しょ	
ちゃ	cha	ちゃ	
ちゅ	chu	ちゅ	
ちょ	cho	ちょ	
ひゃ	hya	ひゃ	
ひゅ	hyu	ひゅ	
ひょ	hyo	ひょ	

ぎゃ	gya	ぎゃ	
ぎゅ	gyu	ぎゅ	
ぎょ	gyo	ぎょ	
じゃ	ja	じゃ	
じゅ	ju	じゅ	
じょ	jo	じょ	
にゃ	nya	にゃ	
にゅ	nyu	にゅ	
にょ	nyo	にょ	
びゃ	bya	びゃ	
びゅ	byu	びゅ	
びょ	byo	びょ	

ISBN 9780170403948

ぴゃ	pya	ぴゃ	
ぴゅ	pyu	ぴゅ	
ぴょ	pyo	ぴょ	
りゃ	rya	りゃ	
りゅ	ryu	りゅ	
りょ	ryo	りょ	

みゃ	mya	みゃ	
みゅ	myu	みゅ	
みょ	myo	みょ	

2 Read the words aloud, paying attention to the combination sounds.

a) びょういん (hospital) びよういん (hairdresser)

b) ひょう (hail) ひよう (cost)

c) じゅう (ten) じゆう (free)

d) りゅうがく (student exchange) りゆう (reason)

3 Circle or highlight two errors in each word, and then rewrite the word correctly.

a) **be n kyo u** (study)

ぺ ん き よ う

b) **kyo u ka sho** (textbook)

ぎ ょ う か し よ

c) **shu ku da i** (homework)

し ょ く た い

d) **re n shu u** (practice)

わ ん し ゃ う

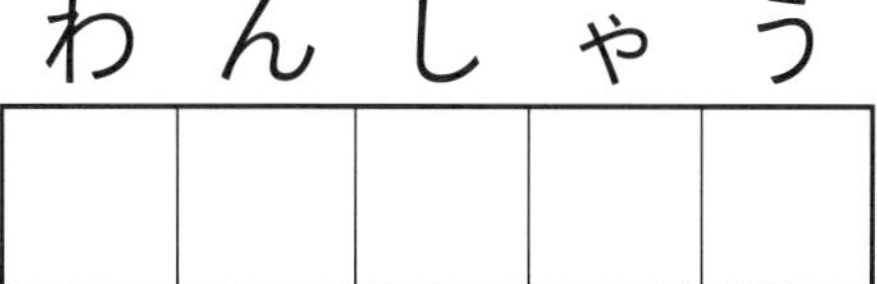

e) **ju gyo u** (lesson)

し ゅ ぎ よ う

f) **chu u ga ku** (junior high school)

ち ゃ う か く

16

4 Highlight the combination sounds, and then match the words to the professions.

ⓐ いしゃ	**ka shu** (singer)
ⓑ しゅふ	**sho u bo u shi** (fireman)
ⓒ きょうし	**kyo u shi** (teacher)
ⓓ かしゅ	**shu fu** (housewife)
ⓔ しょうぼうし	**i sha** (doctor)

5 Fill in the speech bubbles in the cartoon.

ISBN 9780170403948

6 Write the words in *hiragana*.

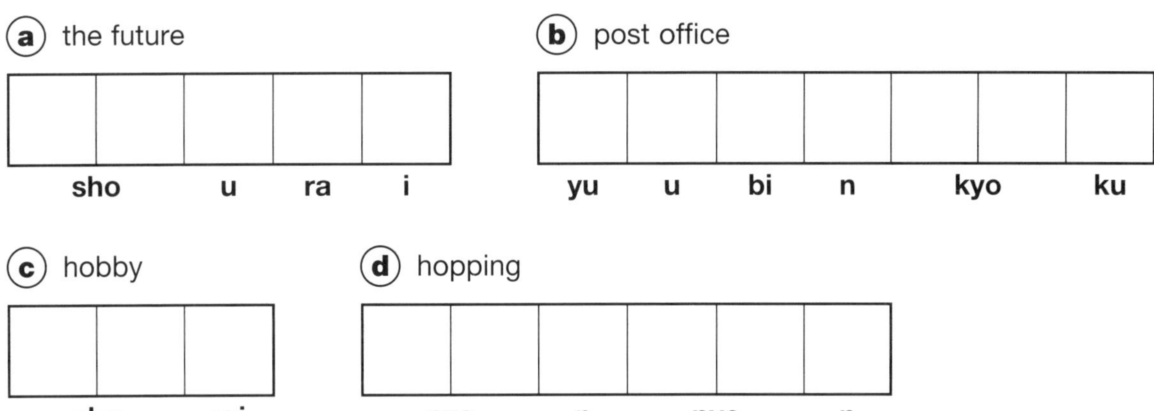

7 Listen to your teacher or watch the Level 16 dictation video. Write the words in *hiragana* in the first squares as you hear them. Then, use the extra squares to practise writing the words again.

Take care to write small や, ゆ and よ about one-quarter of the size of regular *hiragana*.

a

b

c

d

e

f

g

h

i

16

ISBN 9780170403948

Level 17: Double consonants

A small つ is a very useful *hiragana* because it can be used to make double consonants in Japanese.

You do not pronounce つ when it is small. You just pause before you say the next sound. For example, まっすぐ (straight ahead) is said as *ma* (pause) *su gu*.

When writing the sounds made by small つ in *romaji*, the first letter of the following sound is repeated. For example, っす becomes *ssu*, and まっすぐ is written as *massugu*.

1. Read the words aloud, paying attention to small つ. Remember that you do not pronounce small つ.

a	ねこ (cat)	ねっこ (root)
b	きて (て-form of 'come')	きって (stamp)
c	みつ (syrup)	みっつ (three things)
d	ちょうど (just, exactly)	ちょっと (a little)

2. Practise writing small つ. Use the dotted lines to help you place your small つ correctly in the bottom-left of each square.

っ	っ	っ									

3. Unjumble the *hiragana* words and rewrite them correctly.

a	**na tto u** (fermented soy bean)	うなっと	
b	**bi kku ri** (surprise)	っくりび	
c	**i ppa i** (a lot)	ぱいいっ	
d	**sa ppo ro** (Sapporo, a city name)	さろっぽ	
e	**so kku ri** (look alike)	くっりそ	

ISBN 9780170403948

4 General counting words are used to count things that do not have specific counting words, such as food and questions.

Write each general counting word. Then, read them aloud, paying attention to small and big つ.

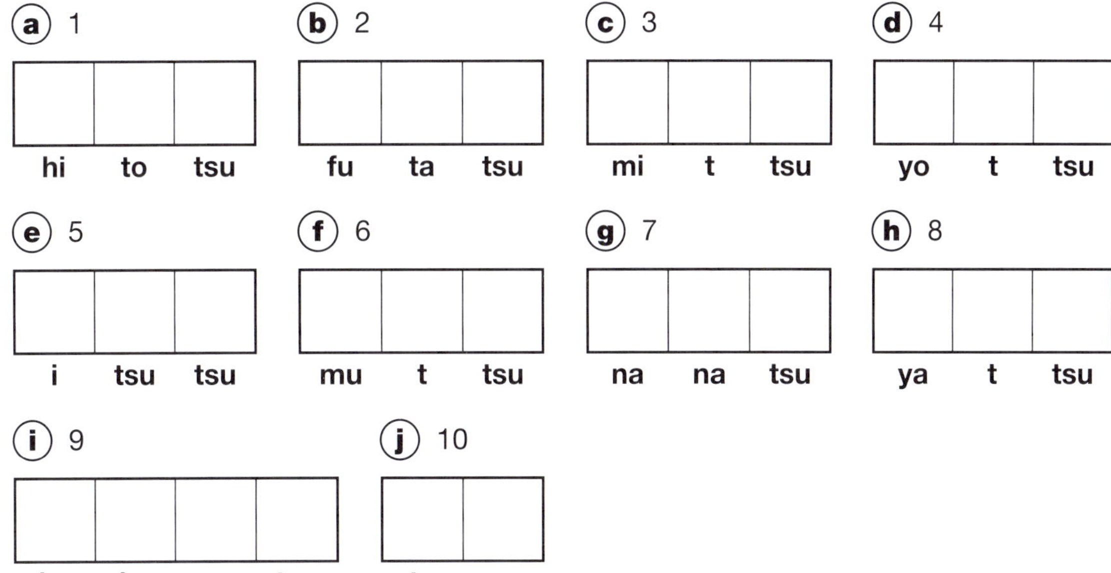

5 Write the classroom expressions in *hiragana*.

a Please stand up.

b Please sit down.

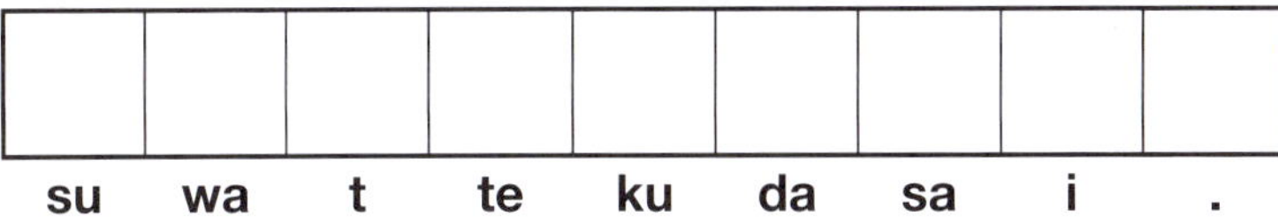

6 Listen to your teacher or watch the Level 17 dictation video. Write the words in *hiragana* in the first squares as you hear them. Then, use the extra squares to practise writing the words again.

a  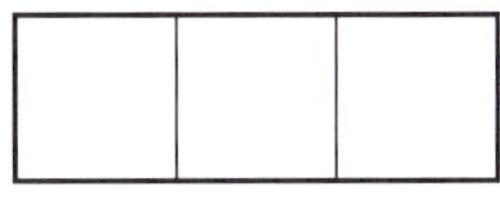 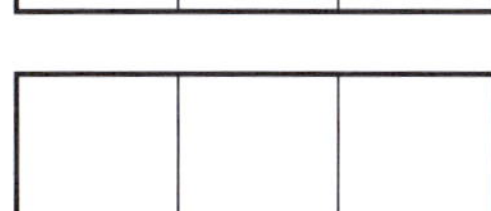

b

c

 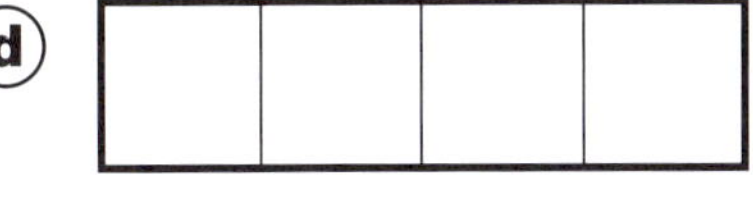 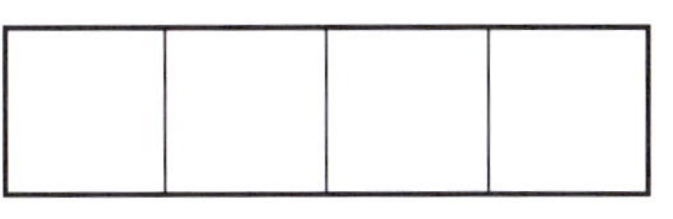 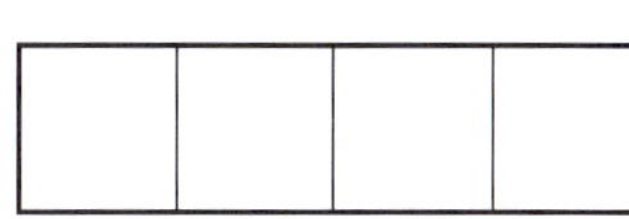

 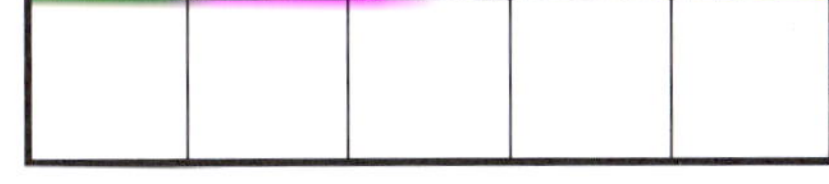 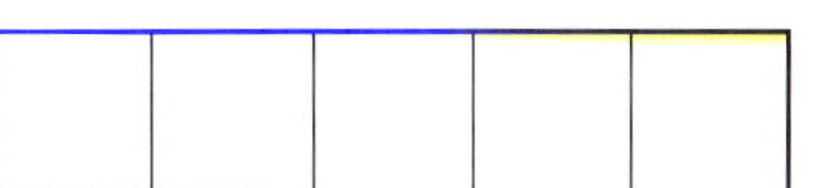

17

ISBN 9780170403948

Level 18: Monster puzzle

Write the words in *hiragana* and then find them in the puzzle. Remember to look in every direction, including diagonally and backwards

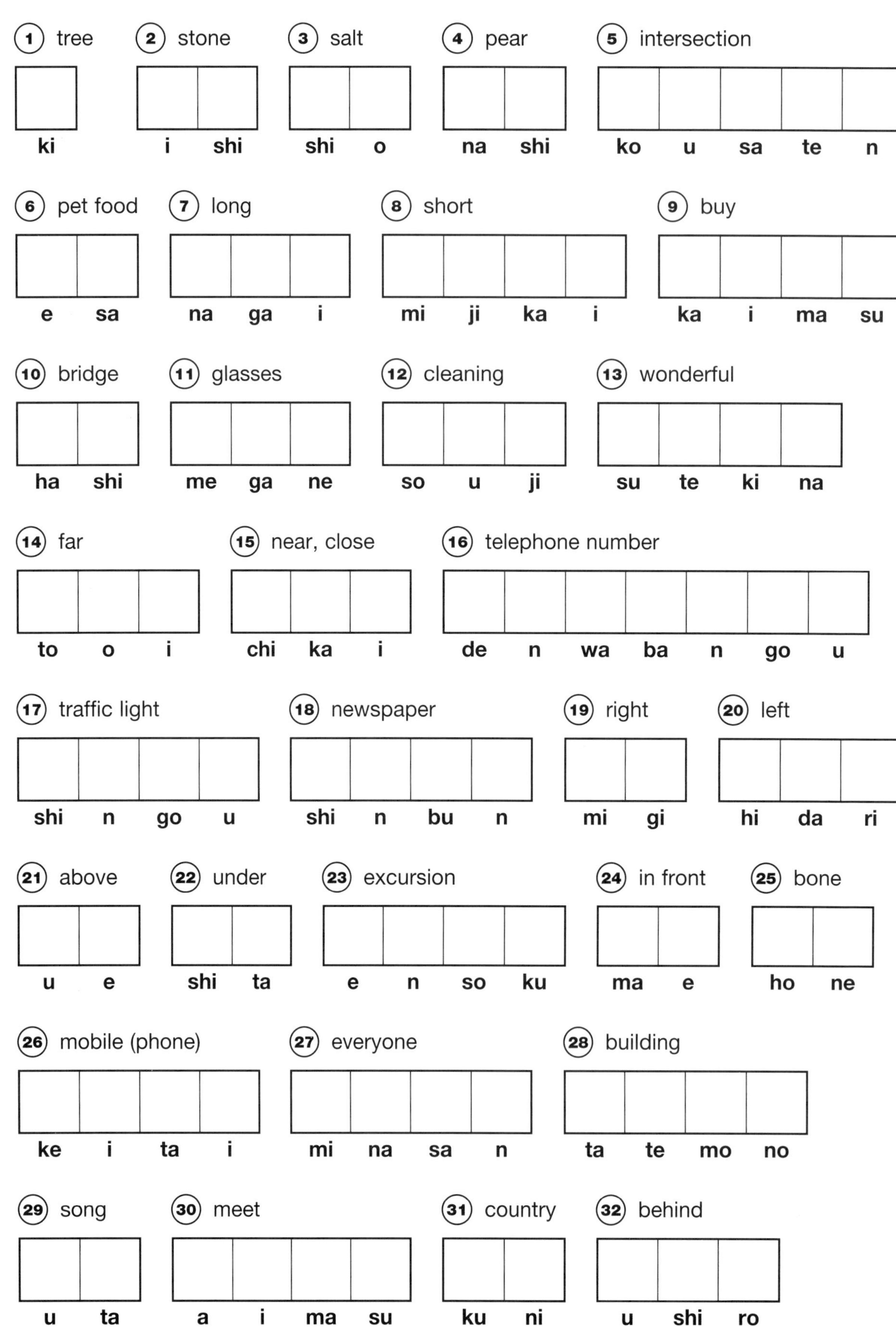

ISBN 9780170403948

り	け	い	た	い	ざ	う	た	に	や	ま	え
き	ご	と	ら	ぐ	だ	し	ば	ひ	し	お	ほ
ゆ	そ	る	う	え	け	ろ	せ	み	な	さ	ん
ぎ	ふ	う	で	ん	わ	ば	ん	ご	う	と	な
し	い	て	じ	れ	ぐ	ぱ	ず	ふ	ん	し	む
ん	へ	を	か	い	ま	す	ね	た	て	も	の
ぶ	ぞ	く	ぷ	ゆ	ら	か	が	を	さ	り	て
ん	じ	に	め	ぬ	す	て	き	な	う	ゆ	げ
す	ら	ぴ	が	も	ま	な	す	ら	こ	ぽ	と
な	と	む	ね	の	い	こ	え	し	た	ひ	え
ぎ	お	び	り	ぐ	あ	い	さ	ぼ	だ	れ	ん
は	い	か	ち	わ	そ	ろ	か	り	ぺ	は	そ
な	が	い	ち	よ	せ	ほ	に	じ	や	し	く
ざ	ら	う	ご	ん	し	ね	ぬ	ぞ	み	ぎ	よ

18

ISBN 9780170403948

Level 19: Vertical writing 2

When written vertically, small つ, や, ゆ and よ are written in the top-right of the square, in the same position as full stops and commas.

1. Copy the example sentences, paying attention to the position of small characters and punctuation marks.

Let's buy ten tickets.

きっぷをじゅうまい
かいましょう。

Junior high school is fun.

ちゅうがっこうは、
たのしいです。

Let's try a challenge!

(a) Highlight or circle です in the text. What do you notice about where です appears in each sentence?

____

(b) How many times can you find わたし?

____

わたし の ともだち は まりこさん です。まりこさん は
１４さい です。とても やさしい です。よく いっしょ に
えいが を みます。そして すいえい も します。でも、
わたし は すいえい が とくいじゃない です。

ISBN 9780170403948

Level 20: Particles

Particles are used in Japanese to organise words in sentences and to communicate meaning. Without particles, you just have words. Particles tell readers the role of each word in a sentence.

Particle は

The particle は indicates the main topic of a sentence. It is pronounced *wa* but spelt は.

When the sound *wa* is part of a word, it is spelt わ. When the sound *ha* is part of a word, it is spelt は.

Look at the example to see the pronunciation difference.

ha chi	wa	ka wa i i		
はち	は	かわいい	です。	(Bees are cute.)
word	particle	word	word	

Particle を

In Level 12, you learnt that there are two *o* sounds in the *hiragana* chart: お is used to write words, and を is a particle.

The particle を indicates the object of a verb or the activity being done.

Read the example to understand how お and を are used in Japanese.

o ka shi	wo		
おかし	を	たべます。	(I eat sweets.)
word	particle	word	

To make the distinction clearer, we use *wo* instead of *o* to indicate the particle in *romaji* or *furigana*; however, they are pronounced the same.

Particle へ

This particle indicates a destination or place that we are moving to or from. We pronounce it as *e* even though it is written as へ.

When they are part of a word, the *e* sound is spelt え and the *he* sound is spelt へ.

You can see the different pronunciations of へ in the following sentence.

he ya	e	ka e ri ma su	
へや	へ	かえります。	(I will go back to my room.)
word	particle	word	

1 Choose the correct *hiragana* to complete the sentences.

a I am 13 years old.

(わ、は)		(わ、は)		
☐たし		☐	13さい	です。
word		particle	word	word

b I eat rice balls.

(お、を)	(お、を)	
☐にぎり	☐	たべます。
word	particle	word

c I will go to the station.

(え、へ)	(え、へ)	
☐き	☐	いきます。
word	particle	word

20

ISBN 9780170403948

Level 21: Let's write

Greetings and useful expressions あいさつと よく つかう ひょうげん

(a) Good morning.

o ha yo u go za i ma su .

(b) Good afternoon. (Hello.)

ko n ni chi ha* .

*Pronounced as *wa* but written as *ha*.

(c) Goodbye.

sa yo u na ra .

(d) Thank you.

a ri ga to u go za i ma su .

(e) You are welcome.

do u i ta shi ma shi te .

(f) See you tomorrow.

ma ta a shi ta .

(g) Excuse me.

su mi ma se n .

(h) How do you do?

ha ji me ma shi te .

(i) Nice to meet you.

do u zo yo ro shi ku .

(j) Thank you. (Said before eating.)

i ta da ki ma su .

(k) Thank you. (Said after eating.)

go chi so u sa ma de shi ta .

Japanese study にほんご の べんきょう

(a) Japanese language

ni ho n go

(b) *hiragana*

hi ra ga na

(c) *kanji*

ka n ji

(d) textbook

kyo u ka sho

(e) vocabulary

ta n go

(f) grammar

bu n po u

(g) conversation

ka i wa

(h) essay

sa ku bu n

(i) revision

fu ku shu u

ISBN 9780170403948

Family かぞく

My family わたし の かぞく

Use these words when you are talking about your own family.

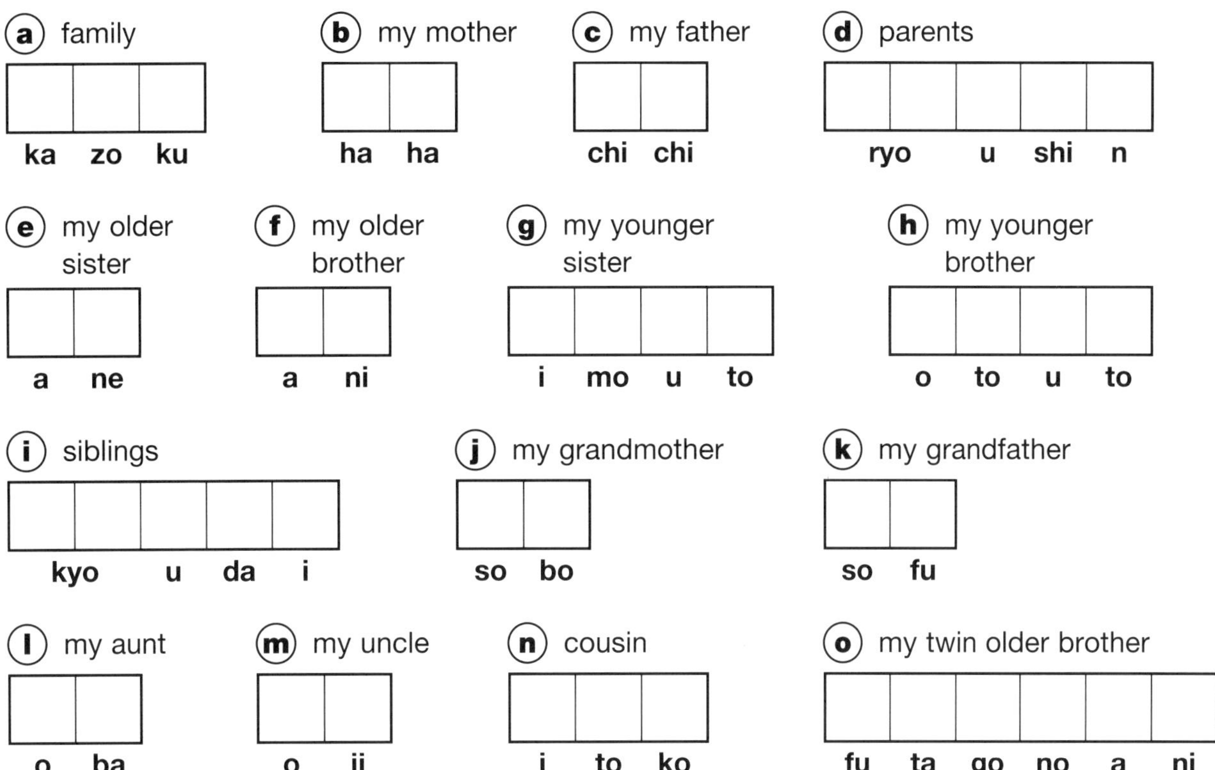

Someone else's family ほか の ひと の かぞく

Use these words when you are talking about someone else's family and when you are addressing your own family.

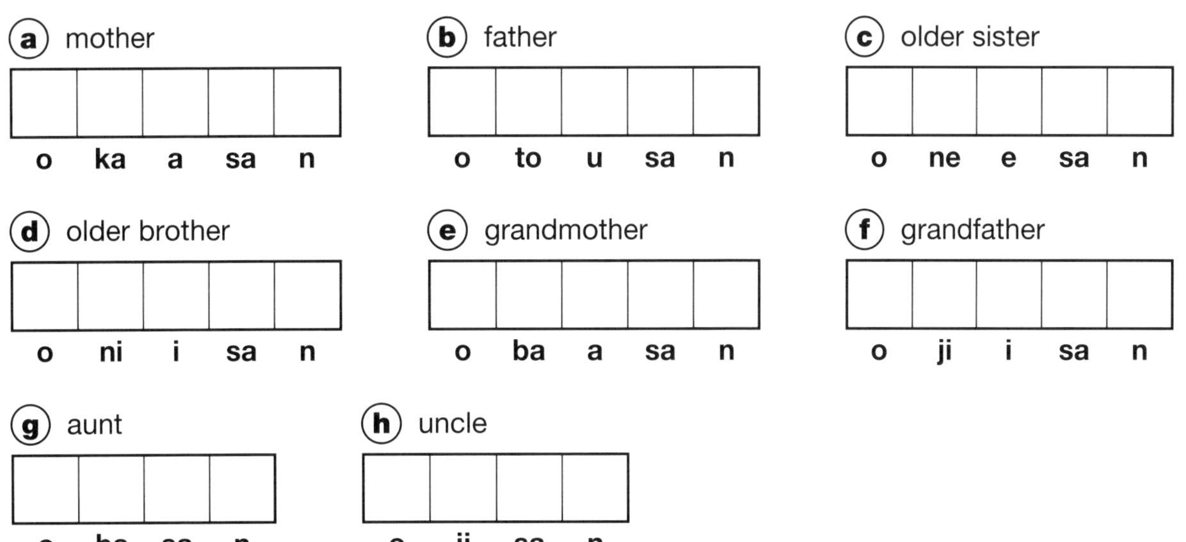

These two words are only used when talking about someone' else's family.

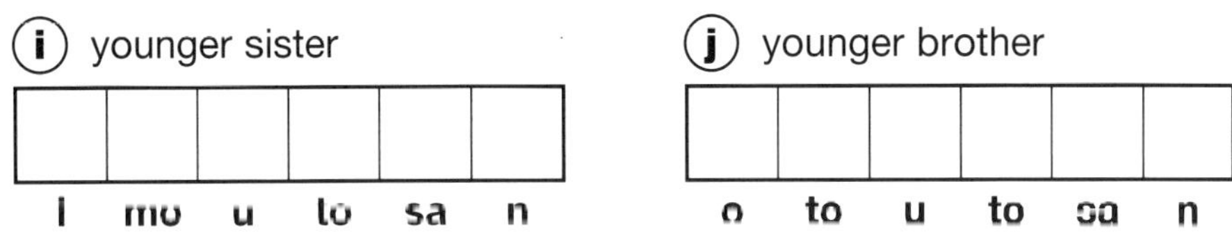

21

ISBN 9780170403948

Food and drinks たべもの と のみもの

(a) food
ta be mo no

(b) drinks
no mi mo no

(c) cooked rice, meal
go ha n

(d) vegetables
ya sa i

(e) fish
sa ka na

(f) meat
ni ku

(g) fruit
ku da mo no

(h) egg
ta ma go

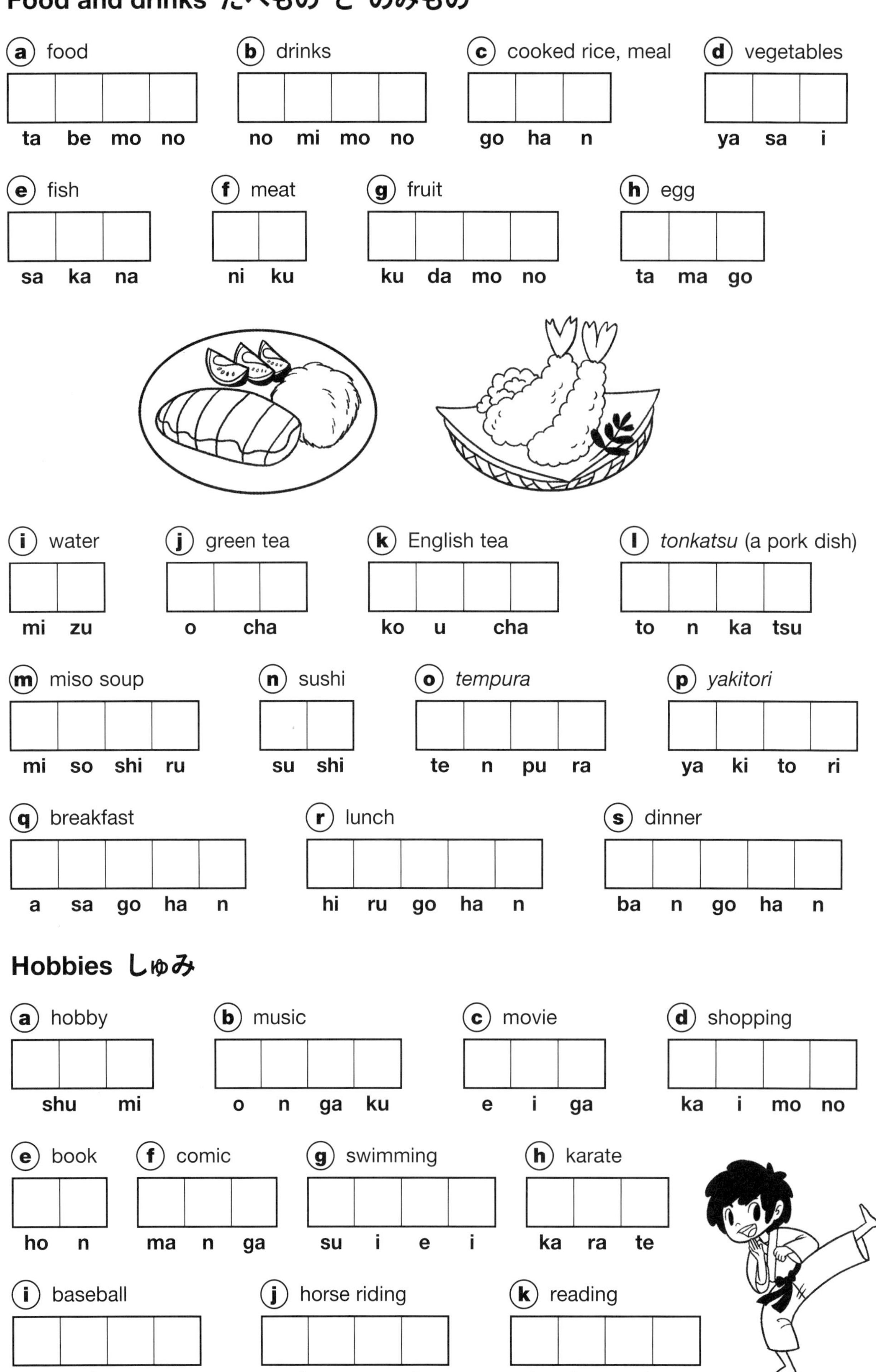

(i) water
mi zu

(j) green tea
o cha

(k) English tea
ko u cha

(l) *tonkatsu* (a pork dish)
to n ka tsu

(m) miso soup
mi so shi ru

(n) sushi
su shi

(o) *tempura*
te n pu ra

(p) *yakitori*
ya ki to ri

(q) breakfast
a sa go ha n

(r) lunch
hi ru go ha n

(s) dinner
ba n go ha n

Hobbies しゅみ

(a) hobby
shu mi

(b) music
o n ga ku

(c) movie
e i ga

(d) shopping
ka i mo no

(e) book
ho n

(f) comic
ma n ga

(g) swimming
su i e i

(h) karate
ka ra te

(i) baseball
ya kyu u

(j) horse riding
jo u ba

(k) reading
do ku sho

ISBN 9780170403948

Places ばしょ

ⓐ school

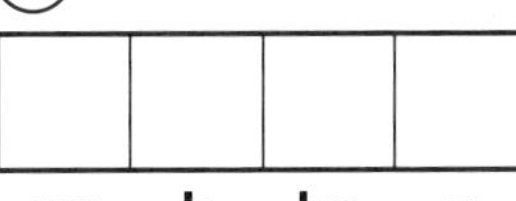

ga k ko u

ⓑ home

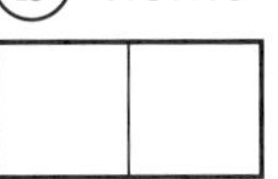

u chi

ⓒ friend's home

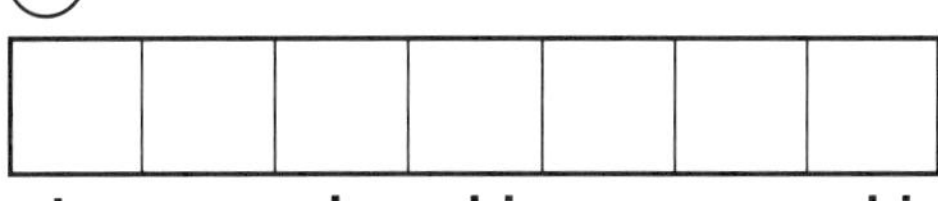

to mo da chi no u chi

ⓓ beach

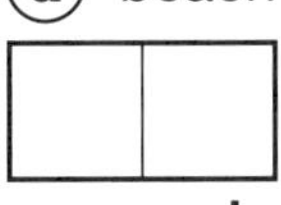

u mi

ⓔ city, town

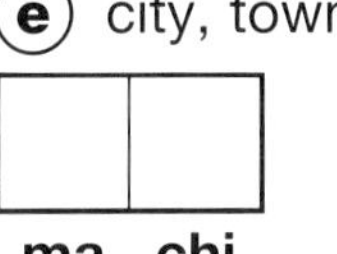

ma chi

ⓕ station

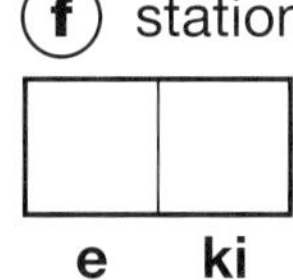

e ki

ⓖ park

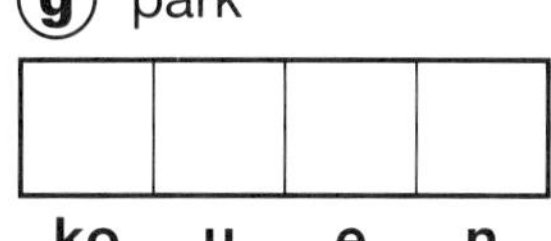

ko u e n

ⓗ shop

mi se

ⓘ garden

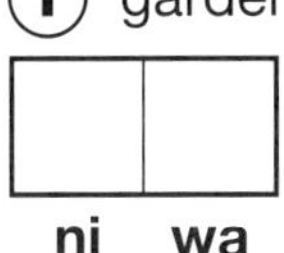

ni wa

ⓙ mountain

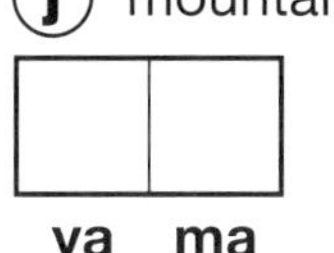

ya ma

ⓚ river

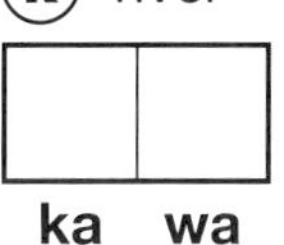

ka wa

ⓛ Shinto shrine

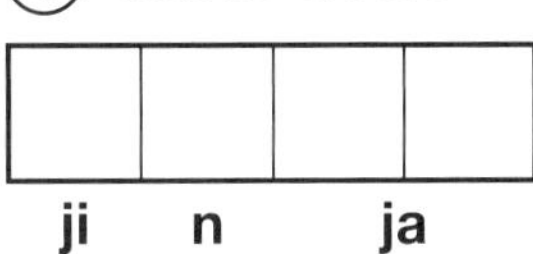

ji n ja

ⓜ temple

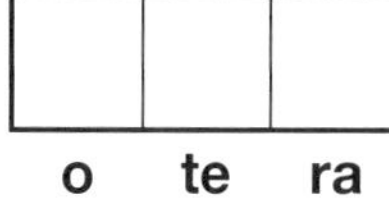

o te ra

Animals どうぶつ

ⓐ dog

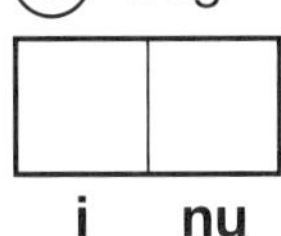

i nu

ⓑ cat

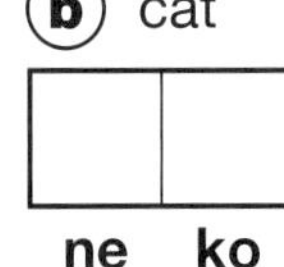

ne ko

ⓒ bird

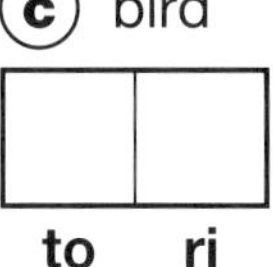

to ri

ⓓ horse

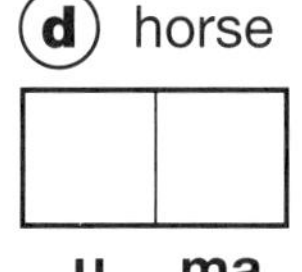

u ma

ⓔ fish

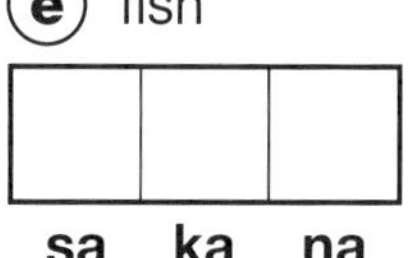

sa ka na

ⓕ cow

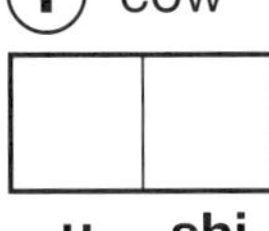

u shi

ⓖ snake

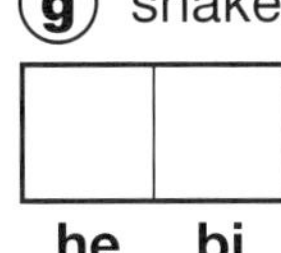

he bi

ⓗ duck

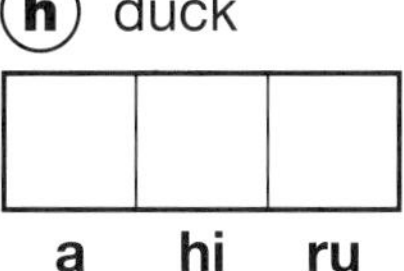

a hi ru

ⓘ mouse

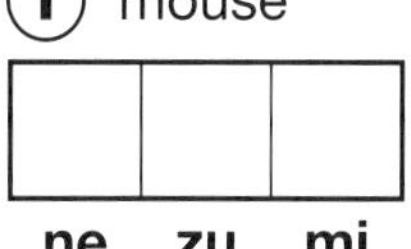

ne zu mi

ⓙ goldfish

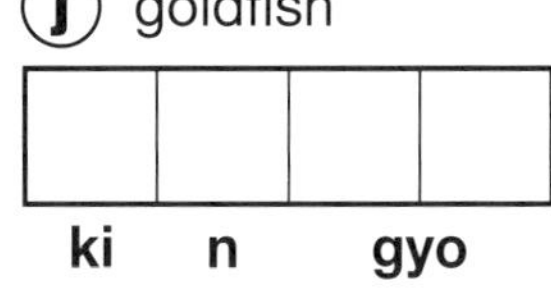

ki n gyo

ⓚ sheep

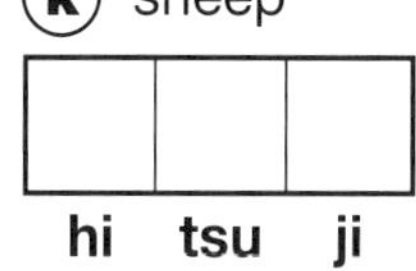

hi tsu ji

21

ISBN 9780170403948

Subjects かもく

(a) Japanese
ni ho n go

(b) English
e i go

(c) mathematics
su u ga ku

(d) music
o n ga ku

(e) science
ka ga ku

(f) history
re ki shi

(g) geography
chi ri

(h) visual art
bi ju tsu

(i) home economics
ka te i ka

(j) physical education
ta i i ku

(k) design and technology
gi ju tsu

Verbs どうし

(a) go
i ki ma su

(b) eat
ta be ma su

(c) drink
no mi ma su

(d) look, watch
mi ma su

(e) read
yo mi ma su

(f) write
ka ki ma su

(g) make
tsu ku ri ma su

(h) open
a ke ma su

(i) close
shi me ma su

(j) listen, ask
ki ki ma su

(k) come
ki ma su

(l) do
shi ma su

(m) do not do
shi ma se n

(n) did
shi ma shi ta

(o) did not do
shi ma se n de shi ta

(p) let's do
shi ma sho u

ISBN 9780170403948

Adjectives けいようし

(a) big

o	o	ki	i

(b) small

chi	i	sa	i

(c) good

i	i

(d) bad

wa	ru	i

(e) delicious

o	i	shi	i

(f) tastes awful

ma	zu	i

(g) expensive, tall

ta	ka	i

(h) cheap

ya	su	i

(i) interesting

o	mo	shi	ro	i

(j) fun

ta	no	shi	i

(k) boring

tsu	ma	ra	na	i

(l) hot

a	tsu	i

(m) cold

sa	mu	i

(n) cute

ka	wa	i	i

(o) scary

ko	wa	i

(p) easy, kind

ya	sa	shi	i

(q) difficult

mu	zu	ka	shi	i

(r) noisy

u	ru	sa	i

(s) pretty, clean

ki	re	i	na

(t) quiet

shi	zu	ka	na

(u) bustling

ni	gi	ya	ka	na

(v) convenient

be	n	ri	na

(w) famous

yu	u	me	i	na

21

ISBN 9780170403948

Level 22: Typing in Japanese

When you type most *hiragana* in Japanese, you just type the sound and the correct *hiragana* appears. For example, if you type 'a', あ appears. If you type 'ki', き appears.

Typing some characters, however, can be a bit tricky.

- The particle は is pronounced as *wa* but needs to be typed as 'ha' so the correct *hiragana*, は, appears.
- The particle へ is pronounced as *e* but needs to be typed as 'he' so the correct *hiragana*, へ, appears.
- For particle を, type 'wo'.
- For ん, you need to type 'nn', or double 'n'.

Combination sounds

When typing combination sounds, you can usually type the first consonant followed by 'ya', 'yu' or 'yo'. For example:

- きゃ – type 'kya'
- にゅ – type 'nyu'
- みょ – type 'myo'.

However, combination sounds with 'sh', 'j' and 'ch' are a bit easier:

- しゃ – type 'sha'
- じゅ – type 'ju'
- ちょ – type 'cho'.

Double consonants

To type a small つ in *hiragana*, type the first sound of the next *hiragana* twice:

- がっこう – type 'ga **k** ko u'
- まっすぐ – type 'ma **s** su gu'.

Small *hiragana*

A small version of any *hiragana* appears if you type 'x' immediately before the sound.

1 Which keys on your keyboard would you use to type these words?

(a) I read a newspaper.

しんぶんをよみます。

(b) Please wait a moment.

ちょっとまってください。

ISBN 9780170403948

Dictation answers

English meanings are given to help students' vocabulary.

Level 1 p. 2

- ⓐ あお blue
- ⓑ あう meet (plain form)
- ⓒ うえ above
- ⓓ え picture
- ⓔ おい nephew

Level 2 p. 5

- ⓐ えき station
- ⓑ かく write (plain form)
- ⓒ こけ moss
- ⓓ こい carp
- ⓔ きかい machine

Level 3 p. 7

- ⓐ いがく medical science
- ⓑ かぎ key
- ⓒ かぐ furniture
- ⓓ かげ shadow
- ⓔ あご chin

Level 4 p. 9

- ⓐ あさ morning
- ⓑ せき seat
- ⓒ あそこ over there
- ⓓ すこし a little
- ⓔ すいか watermelon

Level 5 p. 12

- ⓐ きじ article
- ⓑ ざしき *tatami* room
- ⓒ かぜ wind
- ⓓ かず number
- ⓔ きぞく aristocracy

Level 6 p. 15

- ⓐ たかい expensive, tall
- ⓑ しごと work
- ⓒ した under, below
- ⓓ あいさつ greeting
- ⓔ ちかてつ underground train

Level 7 p. 17

- ⓐ てつだい help
- ⓑ であい encounter
- ⓒ どこ where
- ⓓ どきどき heart racing
- ⓔ でし disciple

Level 8 p. 19

- ⓐ なに what
- ⓑ いぬ dog
- ⓒ にく meat
- ⓓ おかね money
- ⓔ えのぐ paints

Level 9 p. 23

- ⓐ はな flower
- ⓑ ふね ship
- ⓒ へたな bad at
- ⓓ ひざ knee
- ⓔ ほそい thin

Level 10 p. 26

- ⓐ そば nearby, beside
- ⓑ ぼく I (boys)
- ⓒ へび snake
- ⓓ かべ wall
- ⓔ ぶかつ club activities
- ⓕ ぽつぽつ in small drops
- ⓖ ぷくぷく chubby

Level 11 p. 30

- ⓐ やま mountain
- ⓑ あめ rain
- ⓒ ゆき snow
- ⓓ つよい strong
- ⓔ のみもの drinks
- ⓕ むずかしい difficult

Level 12 p. 34

- ⓐ おふろ bath
- ⓑ でんわ telephone
- ⓒ うるさい annoying, noisy
- ⓓ うれしい happy
- ⓔ べんりな convenient
- ⓕ あたらしい new

Level 15 p. 41

- ⓐ きいろ yellow
- ⓑ せんせい teacher
- ⓒ ぎんこう bank
- ⓓ おおきい big
- ⓔ おばあさん grandmother
- ⓕ にちようび Sunday

Level 16 p. 45

- ⓐ きんぎょ goldfish
- ⓑ ちゃいろ brown
- ⓒ りゅうがく student exchange
- ⓓ じてんしゃ bicycle
- ⓔ しゅうまつ weekend
- ⓕ りょうしん parents
- ⓖ じんじゃ Shinto shrine
- ⓗ やきゅう baseball
- ⓘ きょうだい siblings

Level 17 p. 47

- ⓐ ざっし magazine
- ⓑ にっき diary
- ⓒ しっぽ tail
- ⓓ がっこう school
- ⓔ かっこいい cool, good-looking

Answers

Level 2 Task 3 p. 4

Start

あ	い	う	あ	か	き	く	け	あ	お	く	か
い	お	お	え	え	う	か	あ	お	か	う	え
え	い	う	い	お	か	こ	く	か	き	く	け
お	う	え	い	い	け	き	け	い	く	こ	え
か	あ	え	け	こ	こ	く	う	え	お	か	あ
か	う	い	お	こ	け	え	き	い	き	か	お
い	か	え	き	あ	い	か	え	お	け	き	い
け	く	お	う	け	き	う	こ	く	か	あ	け
う	い	お	あ	い	あ	お	き	う	う	き	お
く	こ	か	け	け	え	こ	き	お	か	く	え
あ	け	く	う	え	お	こ	け	き	あ	こ	け
う	え	お	け	く	い	お	あ	い	お	き	こ

Goal

Level 3 Task 2 p. 7

が	え	げ	き
け	い	ご	ぐ
き	ご	こ	ぎ
い	か	が	く

Level 4 Task 5 p. 10

い	す	あ	し	か	さ	お	か	う	し	あ	い
か	お	こ	お	け	こ	あ	か	こ	え	か	け
く	す	し	い	う	き	せ	け	す	け	そ	し
ご	え	け	し	ぐ	き	ぎ	い	き	そ	い	し
か	し	ご	い	く	き	あ	げ	け	い	そ	け
い	け	ぎ	あ	け	い	せ	そ	お	え	が	お
そ	け	し	せ	い	さ	ず	き	き	せ	し	が
お	さ	く	お	え	う	そ	せ	い	げ	い	い

Level 7 Task 2 p. 16

Letter number 3 leads to the treasure island.

Level 8 Task 6 p. 20

			ね	
の	ね			
		ぬ		
	に		な	の
な				

Level 9 Task 4 p. 22

す		す		
	で			な
			が	
か		き		
				つ

なつ が すき ですか。Do you like summer?

Level 9 Task 6 p. 23

あさひ ひきだし しはつ つなひき きふ ふん

Level 10 Task 2 p. 25

ぽ	ぱ	こ	ぺ	こ	ぺ	こ
ば	た	ぴ	か	ぴ	く	ぴ
く	か	ぽ	ぺ	ぱ	か	ぱ
ぽ	ぴ	こ	た	く	ぴ	ぴ
ち	ぷ	ち	ぷ	ぱ	か	ぽ
ぽ	た	ぷ	ち	く	ぴ	ぺ

Level 11 Task 4 p. 29

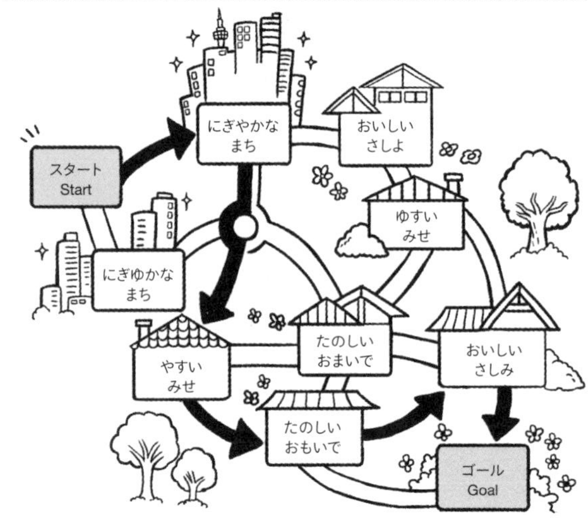

Level 12 Task 6 p. 34

Door number 2 leads to the exit.

Level 15 Task 3 p. 40

どようび　こうえん　えいが

Level 15 Task 5 p. 41

■	■	1 こ	■	2 お	3 お	き	い
4 ぶ	ど	う	■	■	べ	■	■
■	■	5 こ	6 う	え	ん	■	■
■	7 ぼ	う	し	■	8 と	け	い
■	■	■	■	9 ぞ	う	■	■

Level 18 Monster puzzle p. 49

り	け	い	た	い	ざ	う	た	に	や	ま	え
き	ご	と	ら	ぐ	だ	し	ば	ひ	し	お	ほ
ゆ	そ	る	う	え	け	ろ	せ	み	な	さ	ん
ぎ	ふ	う	で	ん	わ	ば	ん	ご	う	と	な
し	い	て	じ	れ	ぐ	ぱ	ず	ふ	ん	し	む
ん	へ	を	か	い	ま	す	ね	た	て	も	の
ぶ	ぞ	く	ぷ	ゆ	ら	か	が	を	さ	り	て
ん	じ	に	め	ぬ	す	て	き	な	う	ゆ	げ
す	ら	ぴ	が	も	ま	な	す	ら	こ	ぽ	と
な	と	む	ね	の	い	こ	え	し	た	ひ	え
ぎ	お	び	り	ぐ	あ	い	さ	ぼ	だ	れ	ん
は	い	か	ち	わ	そ	ろ	か	り	ぺ	は	そ
な	が	い	ち	よ	せ	ほ	に	じ	や	し	く
ざ	ら	う	ご	ん	し	ね	ぬ	ぞ	み	ぎ	よ

Level 22 Task 1 p. 58

(a) shi nn bu nn wo yo mi ma su.

(b) cho tto ma tte ku da sa i.

ISBN 9780170403948